pocket
cornwall

C000064183

Cornwall's Great Houses
and Gardens

Barry Gamble

Alison Hodge

Dedication

To Dad (1927–2011): For his encouragement, and time.

First published in 2014 by
Alison Hodge, 1a Gwavas Road, Newlyn,
Penzance, Cornwall TR18 5LZ, UK
info@alison-hodge.co.uk
www.alisonhodgepublishers.co.uk

Reprinted 2016

ISBN-13 978-0-906720-79-0
British Library Cataloguing-in-Publication Data
A catalogue record for this book is available from
the British Library.

Designed and originated by
BDP – Book Development and Production,
Penzance, Cornwall

Printed in China

Title page: Camelia at Trewidden

Acknowledgements

Thank you to all the owners, managers and gardeners of Cornwall's great houses and gardens who have been so enthusiastically involved in this book. They have pointed out the greatest treasures and advised on when to catch the best plants in bloom. They have been more than generous with their knowledge and time.

A special thank you, too, to Paul Holden of the National Trust for checking the text. I would also like to acknowledge the various published works on Cornish parks and gardens, particularly those by Douglas Ellory Pett (who personally gave me early encouragement) and Timothy Mowl.

Contents

Introduction

Cornwall has an immensely rich historic environment that has attracted considerable attention in recent decades in terms of its conservation, access and presentation. Great houses and gardens have featured significantly in this, and while the National Trust (NT) has long been their prominent guardian there has been an increasing contribution from the many private owners who handle their responsibility of care with equal measures of expertise and passion. A number have increasingly shared their properties with the public, perhaps diversifying their business or maintaining long-standing charitable open days. New trusts have emerged, tackling costly garden restoration through placing visitors at the heart of their ongoing financial sustainability.

Cornish gardens, in particular, have experienced a surge in interest in recent years, contributing substantially to the local economy and being an important part of the tourism offer, particularly in spring when many are at their best. The formation of the Cornwall Gardens Trust, launched in 1988, brought together a wealth of expertise in its strategic and diverse committee, and since that time English Heritage has doubled the number of Cornish gardens in its Register of Parks and Gardens of Special Historic Interest in England. The Cornwall Garden Society, too, continues a tradition that began in 1832 with the Royal Horticultural Society of Cornwall. Its contribution in sustaining the profile and interest in Cornish gardens culminates annually with its outstanding Spring Flower Show held at Boconnoc.

Ten years ago my interest in Cornwall's great houses and gardens became focused because of several jobs that I was working on. First, in 2003, I joined the Bid Team for the Cornwall and West Devon Mining Landscape World Heritage Site as principal author of the nomination to UNESCO's World Heritage List. Great houses, gardens and estates of Cornwall's mineral 'lords', merchants, smelters and mines' 'adventurers' were a component of this cultural landscape and I enjoyed, immensely, working with colleagues who were pioneers of Historic Landscape Characterisation in the then Cornwall Archaeological Unit of Cornwall County Council. At that time, while delving into the history of various properties, apart from inheritance and the wealth derived from marriage dowries and the like, the scale of the links with the mining industry as a source of staggering revenue became apparent. Mineral rights, for example, that were the property of the landowning interests, were leased to companies of 'adventurers' in return for a royalty of a given proportion of the ore raised. Surges of income showered upon the lucky ones, often without investment, anxiety or risk of any kind. Successful industrialists made vast sums too, becoming the *nouveaux riches* of the eighteenth and nineteenth centuries. Income fluctuated with time, of course, and this pattern can often be correlated with extravagant constructions, extensions or embellishments to property that were easily possible in Cornwall's industrial heyday, particularly of copper mining and tin smelting. Sponsorship of plant hunting was a familiar trait, too, that characterized the period.

Second, in 2003–04, I was involved with an exhibition for the Royal Cornwall Museum, entitled Travelling Trees – part of the bicentenary celebrations of the Royal Horticultural Society in 2004. After conducting initial research I began to refine the design concept together with Caroline Dudley OBE (then Director of RCM), my design colleague Colin Fearon, and that most talented writer, and friend, Jacquey Visick who was tragically killed in January 2005. The enthusiasm that I shared with Jacquey on our various visits to meet garden owners and their staff was an inspiration for me to continue where I left off. The following year I worked on the new Abbey Garden Visitor Centre on Tresco, with Curator Mike Nelhams. During my numerous visits to the Scillies his energy, knowledge and passion for the subject were infectious.

The photographs in this book represent a snapshot taken during the last five years. Where useful, for reasons of scale, clarity of structure, setting, or sheer aesthetics, I have included a selection of aerial photographs, many taken during the winter months when the often-relict structure of designed landscapes is more readily seen. These were all shot from the open door of a helicopter, giving me the time and ability to compose the picture in order to communicate a particular significance, position for the sun, and so on. I hope that you enjoy all the photographs as much as I have enjoyed taking them, and that this book helps you to learn a little more about yet another special element of Cornwall's rich historic environment.

Barry Gamble, 2014

About this Book

This book contains a personal selection of Cornwall's historic houses and gardens, the majority open to the public with a few that are strictly private and which may, or may not, open for charity days. They are presented as a gazetteer from west to east, a format that was adopted for my books on Cornish mines (*Cornish Mines: St Just to Redruth* and *Cornish Mines: Gwennap to the Tamar*, published in the Pocket Cornwall series in 2011).

Some properties encourage several hours, or even a day, of exploration. Their character and key features are described briefly, in terms of both the 'hard' built landscape of houses and garden structure (that commonly endures), and the 'soft' landscapes of planting (that changes with time). A short, selective, historical account is given, covering, in particular, some of the important people who lived there, together with an indication of the source of their wealth and when and how they created the places that we know and love today. A full history of each property is beyond the scope of this small volume. However, regarding the houses in particular, Peter Beacham's new Pevsner Architectural Guide to Cornwall is published in 2014, and Paul Holden's book on Cornwall's country houses is due in 2016.

Each property's location is given with a reference to an Ordnance Survey Explorer map. For example, **Trengwainton**, OS Explorer 102: SW444315 refers to Ordnance Survey Explorer map 102, grid reference SW444315.

Measurement

Measurements of land are given in hectares (ha). Note that 1 ha = 2.47 acres. Distances are given in miles; other measurements of length and height are in metres (m). Note that 1 m = 3.28 feet, or 1.09 yards; 1 mile = 1.61 km.

Abbreviations

Compass points are abbreviated as follows: **E** – east; **N** – north; **NE** – north-east; **ENE** – east-north-east … and so on. Other abbreviations used are: **NT** – National Trust; **RHS** – Royal Horticultural Society.

Right: Magnolia.

Abbey Garden, Tresco

OS Explorer 101: SV893142

Tresco is the second largest of the Isles of Scilly: a granite archipelago emerging jewel-like some 24 nautical miles WSW of Land's End. It is host to the sub-tropical Abbey Garden, warmed by the North Atlantic Drift, a powerful ocean current that continues the Gulf Stream NE. Unlike any other garden in Britain, it is said to be like 'the Temperate House at Kew without the glass', or 'Eden with the lid off'. Access to this outstanding 6.9-ha, historic (Listed Grade I) garden is by plane or boat to St Mary's, then by inter-island 'water taxi'.

Tresco is held by the fourth successive generation of the family that first settled here in 1834 and constructed this remarkable garden. There are plenty of facilities, attached to the garden and elsewhere on the island, and it's well worth spending the day, or longer. Don't miss Valhalla, built as a Victorian summerhouse, now a museum of shipwrecked maritime 'art' by Tresco's first garden-maker. It is described by the National Maritime Museum as 'one of the finest collections of merchant ship figureheads in the world.'

Facing: The granite house was built as the home of Augustus Smith (1804–72), who leased the Isles of Scilly as Lord Proprietor. Named Tresco Abbey, it was built in 1835–43, with additions in the early 1860s, and the E tower in 1891 by nephew Thomas Algernon Dorrien Smith (1846–1918), who succeeded him. Standing on a rocky eminence, above the twelfth-century ruins of St Nicholas Priory, it looks across to Star Castle (1593) on St Mary's. Freshwater pools lie to the SE (Abbey Pool, bottom) and N (Great Pool, top right) – considerations, no doubt, for the location of the first 'abbey'. The garden is immediately to the W (centre, left), where planting began in the Well Garden among the Priory ruins. It soon expanded, carving out higher, dryer S-facing terraces. To protect tender plants from frequent salt-laden gales, shelterbelts of Monterey Pine (Pinus radiata) and Monterey Cypress (Cupressus macrocarpa) were planted on the exposed ridges to the N and W, with Holm Oak (Quercus ilex) hedges lower down (from 1890). On these warm terraces, South African and Australian flora thrives. The lower, more humid, flats suit the luxuriant South American and New Zealand species.

The garden has strong axial form imparted by three major E-W walks – Top Terrace, Middle Terrace and Long Walk – intersected by N-S paths, the most prominent being the central Lighthouse Walk culminating in Neptune Steps. In all, there are some 20,000 plants from some 80 countries.

Twin-pointed Gothic arches of the twelfth-century Benedictine St Nicholas Priory (first recorded on Tresco in 1113) that was attached to Tavistock Abbey, dissolved by Henry VIII in 1539. Islanders used it as a cemetery in the eighteenth and early nineteenth centuries, and Augustus began planting in the shelter of its ruins. Today, wall crevices ooze succulent rosettes of aeoniums, most of which are endemic to the Canary Islands, and the vivid chemical mauve and hot pink of mesembryanthemums from South Africa.

Many such species came from Sir William Hooker (1785–1865) of the Royal Gardens at Kew (its first Director in 1841) and his son Sir Joseph (1817–1911), who succeeded him. Sir Joseph, an outstanding botanist and principal confidant of Charles Darwin, remained as Director of Kew until 1885, and the relationship between the Abbey Garden and the Royal Botanic Gardens continues today.

A Century plant (Agave salmiana) on Succulent Cliff above Middle Terrace. This Mexican species was first planted in the Garden in 1894. Blue

Agapanthus praecox subsp. orientalis (Nile Lily) was introduced in 1856; escapees create a spectacular show in the dunes S of the garden.

One of Tresco's iconic trees is the evergreen New Zealand Flame Tree (Metrosideros excelsa), planted in the Abbey Garden from the mid-nineteenth century. Demonstrably salt- and wind-tolerant, it is intolerant of hard frost. New Zealanders call this tree Pohutakawa (= splashed by spray).

King Protea (Protea cynaroides), the national flower of South Africa, belongs to the Proteaceae, one of the earliest groups of flowering plants. They thrive in the Abbey Garden's S-facing, exposed and weathered, well-drained, acid, sandy terrain, favouring such consequent poor levels of nutrients and low available phosphorus.

Trengwainton

OS Explorer 102: SW445315

Trengwainton (= dwelling near the spring or rivulet) is 2 miles NW of Penzance. From the A30 at Heamoor roundabout follow the NT's brown signs: take the B3312 Madron Road, after 550 m turn left at a crossroads into Boscathnoe Lane and continue to Trengwainton's twin entrance lodges (the one on the right dates from 1820, that on the left from 1994 when it was built as a reception, shop and plant sales area). The visitors' car-park is to the right.

The NT owns Trengwainton, a gift of Col. Sir Edward Bolitho in 1961. Its principal shallow-valley woodland garden is narrow and linear, less than ½ mile long by, on average, less than 90 m wide. It slopes gently from the SE to the NW where, at the top, the house (private) looks obliquely across a lawn framed by trees to a stunning vista of St Michael's Mount and the Lizard peninsula beyond (all historic Bolitho houses enjoyed a view of the Mount). Trengwainton is renowned for its exotic plants, particularly magnolias (over 50 varieties), tree ferns and rhododendrons; a number of the latter originate from the Burmese plant-hunting expedition of Kingdon-Ward in 1927–8. Additional woodland and a Georgian brick Walled Kitchen Garden (including a unique series of raised, W-facing, sloping beds) are complemented by a tearoom.

In 1688 Trengwainton passed from Thomas Cowling to Francis Arundell (of Menadarva, descended from a younger son of Sir John Arundell of Trerice [pages 97–8]). It was bought by John Praed of nearby Trevethoe c. 1700 and, in 1814, by wealthy West Indian sugar planter Sir Rose Price (1764–1834). Price enlarged the house and constructed the raised terrace, planted shelterbelts, built the entrance lodge and walled gardens and created pools for fish and wildfowl in the valley, employing black servants on his Cornish estate. Thomas Simon Bolitho (1808–87) acquired Trengwainton in 1867. The Bolithos were successful 'merchant princes of Cornwall' and 'adventurers' who owned banks (eventually part of Barclays), mines, tin smelters, ships and pilchard fisheries. It was from 1925, under Lt.-Col. Sir Edward HW Bolitho (1882–1969, grandson of TS Bolitho), that the era of exotic gardening began.

Facing: Aerial view to the lawn and E front of Trengwainton House across feature drives: Long Walk (centre), Sir Rose Price's former carriageway, and the Lower Drive (1897, right) built by Thomas Robins Bolitho (1840–1925). The House Lawn is separated from fields (left) by a ha-ha, avoiding the use of fencing that would otherwise interrupt the vista to St Michael's Mount.

Above: Classically styled in Cornish granite, Trengwainton House is part eighteenth-century, remodelled in 1810 for Sir Rose Price, and sub-stantially enlarged during the later nineteenth century by the Bolitho family.

Price's family founded Worthy Park Plantation in St Catherine parish, Jamaica, in 1670. When Sir Rose died in 1835, emancipation of slaves in Jamaica was nearly complete and the plantation system came to an end, bringing bankruptcy to countless planters. To settle debts, Trengwainton was sold to the Stephens family of Tregenna Castle, St Ives. The Bolitho family of Penzance bought the estate in 1867 and still live in the house.

Above: Upper Pond, created by the NT in 1997, from the Chinese Bridge. Dazzling pink, fragrant azaleas add a splash of colour to the verdant coolness of tree ferns and aquatic plants.

Left: Statuesque tiers of pink and yellow flowers of candelabra primulas mix with purple iris to create a stunning show of late-spring colour along the border of the Stream Garden. This was created by Sir Edward alongside the Lower Drive in the 1920s, and planted with these moisture-loving plants c. 1950.

Rhododendron, a genus so characteristic of the planting by Sir Edward Bolitho in this very special woodland garden. In 1926 George Johnstone of Trewithen (pages 91–6) offered Lt.-Col. Edward Bolitho (Royal Artillery, retired) a share in the 1927–8 plant-hunting expedition of Frank Kingdon-Ward (1885–1958). From this trip, to NE Assam and the Mishmi Hills of Upper Burma, Kingdon-Ward returned with the seed of over 150 species, including several rhododendrons that flowered for the first time in the UK at Trengwainton. The garden expanded with sound horticultural advice from Johnstone and another historic Cornish garden-maker, John Charles Williams (1861–1939), Edward Bolitho's cousin at Caerhays (pages 106–11).

Trewidden

Trewidden's Camellia Garden comprises a collection of over 300 cultivars – mostly established by Mary Williams – that thrive in its mild wet climate and acid soil.

OS Explorer 102: SW444295

Trewidden lies about 2 miles SW of Penzance and a little over 1 mile S of its near (Bolitho) neighbour, Trengwainton (pages 13–17). Take the A30 towards Land's End and turn off right (N) approx. 230 m before Buryas Bridge. A long (550-m) drive, much of it lined with high granite hedges, ascends the hill to the property. A car-park, tearoom and excellent plant sales area mark the garden entrance some 140 m SW of Trewidden House (private).

Prior to 1830 Trewidden was little more than a small dwelling near the site of an ancient tin mine, an openwork known as Trewidden Bal. Evidence remains in the form of hollows (Tree Fern Pit) and hummocky waste rock dumps (the Burrows, as spoil tips are known in Cornwall). Though the mine has no recorded production, the local Bolitho family were extensively involved in tin mining and smelting at the time (particularly in West

Facing: Looking towards the S entrance front of Trewidden House, built in Tudor Gothic style by Edward Bolitho in the 1840s. White-painted pebbledash over stucco, the complex and irregular plan is thought to be designed to appear as if evolved over a period of time; the L-shaped two-storey range of coach house and stables (converted into studios in 2008) bear a date-stone of 1848. The property remains in the ownership of the Bolitho family, and the house is available year-round to rent as holiday accommodation. The principal garden lies immediately to the W (left).

Penwith) and are sure to have known of the mine's existence. However, the flat 'beds' of tin in granite having been worked out, and with no prospects at depth, the property was purchased in 1830 by Edward Bolitho (1804–90), who chose to make Trewidden his home. The new house was built in the 1840s, to be followed by the walled kitchen

Late-March spectacle of Magnolia x veitchii 'Peter Veitch' towering above the Pond. This deciduous hybrid, a cross between the Himalayan M. campbellii and Chinese M. denudata, produces purple-pink goblet-shaped flowers in spring – before leaf emergence. These most striking magnolias came from a single seedling raised by Peter Veitch (1850–1929) of the Exeter nurseries in 1907. Trewidden's is a 'Champion' tree – the largest in Britain.

Australian tree ferns (Dicksonia antarctica) in the Tree Fern Pit, former openwork of the tin mine known as Trewidden Bal. Head Gardener William Maddern planted these in 1902, having selected them from Treseders' Nurseries that had harvested them in southern Australia four years earlier. John Garland Treseder (1841–1923) founded a nursery business in Sydney, Australia, after migrating from Mylor to Ballarat (with his two brothers) in 1857 to join the Victoria Gold Rush. He was back in Cornwall 1866–76, returned to Sydney and then came back to Cornwall again in 1897. He championed tree ferns in Cornish gardens, his father James Treseder having served under plant hunter William Lobb at Scorrier House, and who first established the family nursery in 1839 in the former vegetable gardens of Enys' Old Mansion House in Truro. Trewidden's Fern Pit is said to contain the best stand in the Northern hemisphere.

garden and plantations that later provided shelter for exotic plants introduced during the 1880s by Edward's son, Thomas Bedford Bolitho (1835–1915). By this time horticultural journals were commenting on the standard of plantings and extensive groves of pines and rhododendrons. He also created the Pond and planted the Tree Fern Pit. Mary Williams (1899–1977), Thomas's daughter, who married Charles Williams of Caerhays, made more notable additions to Trewidden Garden when she moved there in 1955, in particular camellias and magnolias. The Williamses had also lived at Greenway near Dartmouth in Devon, once owned by Edward Carlyon of Tregrehan, which Thomas had purchased in 1882, and which in 1938 became the home of Mrs Max Mallowan (Agatha Christie).

The enchantingly buttressed and gnarled bole of the Dawn Redwood tree (Metasequoia glyptostroboides). This specimen is among the first of this deciduous species (a native of China; the two other metasequoia species, from California, are evergreen) to be introduced into Britain in the first wave of planting that began in 1949. It has the widest girth for its species in Britain.

St Michael's Mount

OS Explorer 102: SW514298

St Michael's Mount, a national treasure and one of Cornwall's most prized jewels, lies 2 miles E of Penzance, 457 m offshore. Park at Marazion; the Mount is accessed by causeway at low tide; otherwise, take a boat ride.

The castle is the official residence of Lord St Levan, whose family, the St Aubyns, have lived here since 1659. In 1954 most of the property was given to the NT, but the family estate retained a 999-year lease to live in the castle and operate the busy visitor business; they also run the popular Island Café. In the island's steep and exposed granite SE quadrant, there is a fine example of maritime subtropical gardening, somewhat 'on the edge'!

St Michael 'the Archangel' is the patron saint of mariners – and 'high places'. Some will make a link between the Mount and its Norman counterpart – Mont Saint-Michel in France. Its similarity as a tidal, conical-shaped rocky island, crowned by a medieval priory castle, is not simply coincidence. Robert de Mortain (c. 1038–95), half-brother of William the Conqueror, gave St Michael's Mount to the Norman Abbey c. 1070, a couple of years before he himself became Earl of Cornwall. Bernard du Bec (died 1149), Abbot of Mont Saint-Michel, ordered the building of a Benedictine priory on St Michael's Mount in 1135, perhaps modelled after his own. The association lasted until 1414 when King Henry V formally appropriated the Mount from its Norman owners. During the War of the Roses (in 1473) the Mount was besieged, and following the Dissolution of the Monasteries (in 1536), Henry VIII had designs on St Michael's Mount as a fortress that, like the priory of the monks before, looked seaward. In 1549 it was seized by Cornish rebels during the Prayer Book Rebellion, and in 1588 the first warning beacon signalling the approach of the Spanish Armada into the English Channel was lit on the Mount. In 1640 it came into the ownership of Royalist Sir Francis Basset (knighted by King Charles I at Boconnoc in 1644, died 1645), and was defended during the Civil War from 1642 to 1646, when it finally surrendered to Parliamentarian forces. Col. John St Aubyn (1613–84) of Clowance was made Captain of the Mount, and in 1659 he purchased it.

Flowering Agave americana create striking silhou-
ettes overlooking the E Terraces.

Facing: NE view to the Mount, showing struc-
tural joints and mineralized sheeted veins in the
rugged and pronounced granite 'stock' (late-
Carboniferous-Permian) that was intruded into
surrounding Devonian sedimentary rock (now
metamorphosed) that forms much of the lower
elevations of the island (left and above centre).
The granite, surmounted by the priory and castle,
rises 67 m above sea level and is host to the most
remarkable situation of any house in England. The
harbour has a fifteenth-century element, but was
remodelled c. 1727 by Sir John St Aubyn (1699–
1744, 3rd Baronet) and largely rebuilt in 1824 by
Sir John St Aubyn (1758–1839, 5th Baronet; five
successive baronets were called Sir John!).

The medieval priory core (centre left) is substantially intact despite Victorian (particularly 1874–80) neo-Gothic accretions (centre right) by architect Piers St Aubyn (1815–95, a cousin of the 1st Baron St Levan). The precipitous cliffs of the SE quadrant of the Mount are a terraced 4-ha garden. In 2009, while a gardener was abseiling here, a Bronze Age 'smith's hoard' was discovered. Walled gardens, thought to have been created by the daughters of Sir John (1726–72, 4th Baronet) in the 1780s, share this suntrap with the E and W Terraces added in the 1870–80s. Exotic flora thrives, including the agapanthus, a native of the Cape Floristic Region, South Africa.

Clowance

Looking N over the lake and parkland to the former seat of the St Aubyn family; theirs from 1380 to 1923, when the remaining family transferred to Pencarrow. When Sir John St Aubyn (1758–1839, 5th Baronet) died in 1839, Clowance passed to his nephew, the Revd John Molesworth (1791–1844), of the Molesworths of Pencarrow, vicar of Crowan. St Aubyn was added to his name; hence Pencarrow is now the home of the Molesworth-St Aubyns.

The classical-style granite house is to the design of architect James Piers St Aubyn (1815–95). It is substantially a rebuild, post-1843, of a predominantly 1770s house that suffered two major fires – in 1837 and 1843. The grounds were replanted in the 1720s (when it also had a deer park), and again in the 1770s by John Nicholls (father of a St Aubyn mistress), a landscape gardener in the style of Lancelot 'Capability' Brown. Like other Cornish estates, Clowance lost much of its earlier woodlands to the mining industry. The St Aubyns made a fortune from mining, including vast royalties from the adjacent Crenver & Wheal Abraham copper mine that they owned. Elements of a grand ornamental landscape remain; the temples and once-famous spar grotto have all but gone.

OS Explorer 104: SW635350

The Clowance Estate is in Crowan parish ½ mile SSW of Praze-an-Beeble (3 miles S of Camborne on the B3303). The five-mile-long estate wall (dating from 1785), punctuated periodically by former entrance drives and gatehouses, is on both the Praze Road to Leedstown and the road to Nancegollan. The property is significant as the St Aubyn seat, and for its associations with St Michael's Mount (pages 23–6) and Pencarrow (pages 133–6). Visitor access is not promoted, but there is self-catering holiday accommodation.

Godolphin

OS Explorer 102: SW601318

Godolphin House and Estate, now NT, are on the lower NE of Godolphin Hill, ¼ mile NW of Godolphin Cross, some 4 miles NW of Helston. A car-park, signed off the Townshend-Godolphin Cross road, leaves a 365-m walk to the house. The 202-ha Estate can also be accessed from here; a short walk up the ancient, narrow slips – a medieval deer course bounded by massive granite walls – leads to the hillside culminating in the 160-m-high Godolphin Hill. On a fine day, a 360° panorama takes in Mount's Bay in the S and St Ives Bay in the N. The massive stone engine house and stack (Leeds' Shaft) of Great Work Mine – a principal source of the Godolphins' wealth – is less than ½ mile SE.

Godolphin is one of Cornwall's most important houses historically and architecturally; the seat of a family whose fortune derived from Cornish tin. They were courtiers, including Sir William (1515–70), Sidney (1645–1712), 1st Earl (a leading British politician under four sovereigns, who became Lord Treasurer) and Francis (1678–1766), 2nd Earl (who introduced the famous Godolphin Arabian – one of three stallions that founded all modern thoroughbred race horses).

The transfer of the Estate from the Godolphins to the (absent) Dukes of Leeds began with the marriage of Lady Mary (1723–64) to Sir Thomas Osborne (1713–89) 4th Duke of Leeds. On her death, it passed to Francis (1751–99), 5th Duke. It was somewhat neglected by later owners: George Osborne (1775–1838), 6th Duke, reduced the house in 1802, and Francis (1798–1859), 7th Duke, demolished a substantial portion in 1850, leasing the remainder. In 1929, Godolphin was sold.

Facing: NE view to rear of the remnant mansion, showing where the main part of the house stood (lower right, formerly enclosing the S side of the courtyard). Forming the N entrance front (top) are the famous seven-bayed Doric colonnades, with paired ranks of great granite pillars and surmounted rooms with Gothic battlements. This probably dates to c.1636 under Sir Francis (1605–67), who succeeded to the Estate in 1613.

The Great Garden was in a rectangular compartment adjoining to the E (right; it is still there and retains the medieval layout).

Penrose Estate

OS Explorer 103: SW642257

Penrose Estate is 1½ miles SW of Helston. Take the B3304 towards Porthleven and turn off at the second left (S) on the bend as you start to ascend Penrose Hill. Left and left again will take you to the car-park.

The inclusion of Penrose is not for its (private) house and gardens but more for the Estate that has been in the care of the NT since 1974. Penrose House and parkland can be appreciated from the Estate walks that include an outstanding five-mile circular walk around Loe Pool. This is Cornwall's

Parts of Penrose House date from the seventeenth century, probably under John Penrose (1600–79); there were Penroses here (John de Penrose) from at least the late-thirteenth century. The last heir to the Penrose Estate, which extended as far as the 'Sithney side' of Porthleven harbour, sold it in 1771 to Hugh Rogers (1719–73) of Helston. The Rogers married into the Bassets (Margaret, daughter of Francis Basset of Tehidy) and other great Cornish families such as the St Aubyns, Rashleighs, Tremaynes and Killigrews. The house is built from elvan (a quartz-porphyry related to granite), killas and granite – a locally distinctive architectural combination – and was remodelled and extended for the Rogers family, mostly in 1776, 1832, 1837 and 1839. In 1974 Lt.-Com. John Rogers (1925–2012) made a gift of the majority of the Estate to the NT. The (private) garden contains exotics such as rhododendron, tree ferns and bamboo; in the parkland there is a bathhouse (1837) and an ornamental bridge (1847). Diverse mixes of trees in the plantations give way to the more salt-tolerant Montereys near the sea.

largest freshwater lake, formed by the natural shingle 'dam' of Loe Bar foiling the River Cober's course to the sea.

View S to Penrose Estate: Penrose House and garden (private, right) with walled kitchen garden, coach house and stables on the W side of the broad, shallow valley leading down to Loe Pool (left). Extensive parkland (there was a deer park in 1785) and woodland lead to The Loe, originally part of the estuary of the River Cober. Loe Bar, which keeps the lake only 180 m from the sea, *is concealed by the hill (top); the sea in Mount's Bay beyond. There are miles of stunning coastline to explore too. Bar Lodge (1898), which uses the same familiar building stone as the House, is a NT holiday cottage in a fantastic location above the Bar. From here, the Squire's 'Right of Wreck' stretched 'As far as a flaming herring barrel might be seen from land on a fair and calm day'!*

Trevarno

OS Explorer 103: SW643303

Trevarno Estate, 2 miles NW of Helston, is strictly private. But it has significant historical associations and a great Victorian garden.

Trevarno is an ancient manor, first recorded in the accounts of the Earldom of Cornwall in 1296 when held by Randulphus de Trevarno. It was subsequently a secondary seat of the Killigrews of Falmouth, the Carminow and Courtney families and, from 1557, belonged to the Arundells. The Olivers (associated with the Bath bun and Bath biscuits) lived here for at least two periods (the early 1700s and lastly 1780–85). Christopher Wallis (1744–1826), a wealthy attorney and mines' adventurer, who acted as Steward for the Cornish estates of Lord Arundell of Wardour (1740–1808), was living at Trevarno probably by the late-1780s. He bought it from Lord Arundell in 1801, and set about improving the grounds. His grandson, Christopher Wallis-Popham (1803–72), inherited Trevarno and became High Sheriff in 1833, enhancing the garden and remodelling the house (1839). William Bickford-Smith (1827–99) of Camborne bought the Estate

View N to Trevarno Manor above the ornamental lake with Victorian Gothic boathouse (1877) in the NW-SE-trending valley below Chynhale. Christopher Wallis-Popham, High Sheriff of Cornwall in 1833, built a new house in 1839 on the site of the centuries-old former house. The architect was George Wightwick (1802–72) of Plymouth;

Trevarno was the first of his Classical houses. External design is remarkably plain, though there was once a granite Doric portico, later removed; its columns lie neatly near the terrace steps. It was extended in the late-1870s by William Bickford-Smith to the design of James Hicks (1846–96) of Redruth, and was reduced in size again in 1980.

Wallis-Popham built the SW-facing terraced walled garden (centre right) in 1838; William Bickford-Smith later added the glasshouses. In 1883 William Bickford-Smith planted no less than 30,000 trees – 120 different species of conifers in the pinetum alone – and built the conservatory greenhouse at the top of the walled garden.

Above: A Chusan palm (Trachycarpus fortunei) towers above spring blossom and red Japanese Maple (Acer palmatum). William Bickford-Smith created these garden terraces overlooking the ornamental lake. The Gothic 'bothy' (potting shed), arranged internally on three levels, houses a boiler that heated glasshouses in the walled garden.

Facing: A magnificent Swamp Cypress (Taxodium distichum) on an island in the lake, seen on a misty, humid, early summer morning. Formerly a millpond, the lake was enlarged and straightened by William Bickford-Smith, who added the neo-Gothic boathouse (right) and, at the other end, a rockery, a 'spar grotto', and perhaps a fernery.

in 1874; William Smith (adding the surname Bickford in 1868) was the grandson of William Bickford (1774–1834), inventor of the miners' safety fuse patented in 1831. The Bickford-Smiths, by the time they came to

Trevarno, headed a global industry that had expanded from the world's first safety fuse factory in Tuckingmill, Camborne. They lived at Trevarno until 1994.

Trelowarren

View NNE, from above the Pleasure Gardens, to the W front of Trelowarren. The chapel (centre) is a c. 1636 rebuild to create a courtyard by Sir Richard Vyvyan (1611–65, 1st Baronet for services to the crown in the Civil War and Restoration). Sir Richard (1732–81), 5th Baronet, remodelled the house in the mid-eighteenth century to the design of Thomas Edwards of Greenwich, and created the Pleasure Gardens. Sir Vyell Vyvyan (1767–1820), 7th Baronet, continued to plant shelterbelts and carriage drives. Sir Richard Rawlinson Vyvyan (1800–79), 8th Baronet, created the formal steps (centre right) up to the Pleasure Gardens and the 450-m raised walk through the woodland. He built the three walled gardens, including Lady Vyvyan's Garden (centre left).

OS Explorer 103: SW721239

Trelowarren's 400 ha are S of the Helford river, 1 mile E of Garras in Mawgan-in-Meneage. The house is of historical and architectural significance; the gardens (under restoration) are not open to the public.

The manor's first recorded owner was Earl Harold Godwinson (1022–66), last Anglo-Saxon king of England and victor of Stamford Bridge in 1066 (but loser at Hastings, where he died in battle a month later). In 1072 Trelowarren passed to Robert de Mortain (1038–95), half-brother of William the Conqueror, along with 248 other Cornish manors. The Vyvyans obtained Trelowarren by marriage in 1427, and remain in residence today.

Bochym Manor

View to the E front (substantially rebuilt in 1851) of the late-medieval Bochym Manor, 1¼ miles NNE of Mullion. Construction is of Lizard serpentine with granite dressing; the manor house was extended in 1699 when the long cross-wing (right) was built. The property is private but some adjacent buildings host holiday lets, including the mid-nineteenth-century coach house and stables (1887 clock tower, left). The other prominent buildings (centre, top) are a two-storey barn and piggery. The garden structure is a rare survival of a relatively unchanged late-seventeenth-century formal garden plan, with three (now lawned) terraces laid out axially along a central path. Elsewhere, remains of waterfalls, ponds, grottos, melon pit and glasshouses survive from mid-nineteenth-century additions under Davey. About ½ mile ENE (on the other side of the A3083), is Bonython Manor, whose gardens are open to the public.

OS Explorer 103: SW691208

Owners of Bochym include John Winslade, a leader of Arundell's 1549 Cornish rebellion.

On his execution, King Edward VI granted the manor to Reginald Mohun, Sheriff of Cornwall, who passed title to the Bellot family, in whose possession the estate remained until 1730. Bochym was briefly in the hands of Sir Harry Trelawney (1687–1762); by 1860 it was the seat of Stephen Davey (1785–1864, JP and Deputy Lieutenant of Cornwall). The Daveys, originally of Redruth, were old mining and smelting associates of the Williams family, Stephen's daughter Elizabeth marrying John Michael Williams of Burncoose in 1852.

Penjerrick

OS Explorer 103: SW778307

Penjerrick lies 2½ miles SW of Falmouth, about 1 mile S of Budock Water. It is the original valley garden of the Fox family, lesser known than its later counterparts, Glendurgan (pages 47–51) and Trebah (pages 42–6) that overlook the estuary of the Helford river, 2 miles S. Access is past an entrance lodge off Penjerrick Hill, opposite the entrance to Penmorvah Manor. A long, curving drive heads SW through a field, but, before reaching an avenue of Monkey Puzzles that herald the house (private), there is limited parking along the verges above the garden gate. Its trusting collection box marks the way in on foot. Be sure to bring waterproof footwear if visiting in anything other than prolonged dry weather: the lower garden, with its pools and streams, lives up to being a 'jungle' more than most.

In 1762, Quaker George Croker Fox (died 1781) established the family as merchants and shipping agents in Falmouth. They were successful in business and society, as industrialists, mining 'adventurers', scientists, merchants and garden-makers. They bought Penjerrick in the late-eighteenth century and developed it as a summer residence, particularly for George Croker's children: Robert Were Fox (1768–1848), George Croker II (1752–1807) and Mary (1751–1839). Robert Were II (1789–1877) became owner of Penjerrick in 1839, retiring there in 1872. He was a scientist, mining geologist, botanist and natural philosopher, a great friend of Prussian explorer and naturalist Alexander von Humboldt (1769–1859) and Sir Joseph Hooker (1817–1911); the latter who seeded Cornwall as the Himalayas-on-sea. Robert experimented with plants, naturalized over 300 species, and married Maria Barclay. They had three children: Anna Maria Fox (1815–97), Robert Barclay Fox (1817–55) and Caroline Fox (1819–71). In 1839, his father put Robert Barclay in charge of Penjerrick, tasking him with enlarging the house, laying out the drive and lodge, and developing the gardens, including digging ponds in the lower garden. After Barclay's death at 38, his sister Anna Maria continued the planting, inheriting on her father's death in 1877. Twenty years later, nephew Robert Barclay II (1845–1934), known as Barclay, inherited Penjerrick.

Penjerrick House lies at the top of the 6-ha garden occupying the NW-SE steep, sheltered valley that ends at Maenporth. This is not the original house of the pioneering Fox gardeners – that was demolished and replaced (on the same site) by this slate-hung property in 1935. The original front (E) terrace, above the Main Lawn, with its magnificent copper beech and Monkey Puzzle, survives, as does a remnant of a fernery and grotto adjoining to the N.

Facing: Monkey Puzzle (Araucaria araucana) with Rhododendron falconeri *on the Main Lawn. The 'Monkey Puzzler' (originally* Araucaria imbricata, Chile Pine*) was commercialized in Britain by the Veitch nursery. William Lobb (1809–64) sent 3,000 seeds from South America, c. 1841, mostly to Veitch, some to Cornish garden-makers.*

The big-leafed Himalayan tree Rhododendron falconeri*, its leathery leaves with gingery velvet undersides and rounded, creamy-yellow flower heads, was a popular introduction to Cornish gardens by Joseph Dalton Hooker (1817–1911)* from his 1847–51 expedition to the Himalayas (he was the first European to collect plants there) and India, sponsored by Sir Charles Lemon. Other famous rhododendron hybrids first raised at Penjerrick include 'Penjerrick' and 'Barclayi'.

Above: Early morning at Tregedna Pond, in the lower garden, overhung by inflorescence of Gunnera manicata*, tree ferns and bamboo. The narrow sunken road of Penjerrick Hill, 90 m SE of the house, divides the garden in two; a footbridge brings you into the wild, jungle-like lower garden.*

Trebah

The house (private) was built c. 1760 for John Nicholls (1731–88) who left it to his nephew William Nicholls (1763–1803). On his death, Peter Brown Harris (1792–1838), another nephew, inherited. His family lived at Trebah until c. 1830, when Charles Fox (1797–1878) became a tenant. When Peter Harris died in 1838, Charles Fox bought the house and garden together with the valley and Polgwidden Cove. It became his main residence from 1851, by which time he had already instigated shelterbelts of Monterey Pine (Pinus radiata), Maritime Pine (Pinus pinaster) and Holm Oak (Quercus ilex). In 1856–7 he built a large red brick house immediately E of the Georgian house. That was destroyed by fire in 1949, leaving only the Georgian house at the head of the valley once more, and a 'lost' garden.

OS Explorer 103: SW768274

Trebah is an original Fox 'valley garden' on the estuary of the Helford river off Falmouth Bay. Restored by the Hibbert family, who arrived in 1981, it was given to the charitable Trebah Garden Trust in 1992. It is brown-signed from the A39, with its neighbour Glendurgan (pages 47–51), at Hillhead Roundabout on the outskirts of Falmouth. From here it's a bit fiddly, but the signs take you on to the old Hillhead Road to near the Argal Reservoir where you turn left at the crossroads and head for Mawnan Smith. Trebah is 1 mile beyond Mawnan, just past the NT's Glendurgan. The 10-ha garden will provide

Trebah's sub-tropical garden occupies a narrow, 460-m-long, lush, wooded valley that drops 60 m N-S and ends at Polgwidden Beach, just the other side of the large pond. Make the beach part of your visit; if you're staying, the Helford Estuary is a great place for sailing.

View from the Lawn Path (immediately below the house) down the valley to the Mallard Pond, the Helford river and the Bosahan hills of the Lizard peninsula beyond. This hazy morning view is crammed with exotic colour, from the yellow foreground of Acacia pravissima to the mass of pink and red Himalayan rhododendrons, some well over 100 years old. Take a stroll down to Polgwidden Beach – it's 457 m to the shingle. This was an embarkation point for the 29th US Infantry Division on their way to Omaha Beach on D-Day. The beach café was once a boathouse, built by Donald Healey (1898–1988), of sports-car fame, who owned Trebah from 1961 to 1971.

an exciting family day out where children are welcomed – a garden of dreams, some say. There's also a great café.

By the time the Fox family came to Trebah, they were hugely successful shipping agents, merchants and industrialists with fin-

*Many of Trebah's trees reach out of the deep ravine to extraordinary heights. The hardy Chusan palms (*Trachycarpus fortunei, *right) are near-15-m British Champions, at least a century old; seed collected by plant hunter Robert Fortune (1812–80) became commercially available in 1860. Charles Fox's daughter, Juliet Backhouse (1826–98), inherited Trebah and continued the extensive planting of exotics, in a natural and wild style, including 300* Dicksonia antarctica *(in 1880), magnolias, camellias and pieris. Rhododendrons were hybridized, including the famous R. 'Trebah Gem' planted in 1900. When she died the estate passed into the ownership of the Hext family, whose extensive planting of exotics spanned 30 years. Visitors in 1935 included a party of the Duke of Cornwall (later King Edward VIII, but never crowned) with Ernest and Wallis Simpson (who later married the former King Edward). Alice Hext, who also created the Mallard Pond for a flock of flamingos, died in 1939. With the war years, the decline began.*

gers in every pie. Charles Fox (1797–1878), who made Trebah his home, was Manager of Perran Foundry (1824–47). This great industrial concern was founded by the family in 1791 and served metal mines from Cornwall to Australia; they built some of the biggest steam engines in the world. The Foxes were top businessmen, Quakers, and believed in helping anyone in need. They had partnered the 'Methodist mining' Williams family in many ventures, particularly in copper mines

and the transport infrastructure required to ship the ore from the mines to the Swansea smelters, including Portreath Plateway and Harbour. They even contracted to build Plymouth Breakwater together. The Foxes only withdrew from this lasting friendly business alliance in the late-1850s, a decade before Cornish copper crashed for ever.

The stream and ponds are forested by around 40 different species of bamboo, some of which regularly grow over 9 m tall in one season alone. In summer, almost 1 ha of hydrangeas (planted in the 1950s to provide cut-flowers for Covent Garden) create a vibrant sea of 'Oxford and Cambridge' blues around Mallard Pond.

Gunnera manicata, a perennial herb first introduced as a garden ornamental from Brazil in 1867, is now ubiquitous in Cornish valley gardens. In summer its umbrella-like leaves provide an exciting adventure for little people. In winter the leaves of its lime-green canopy die back and turn into clumps of brown, swampy mush.

Glendurgan

View N to Valley Head from above Manderson's Hill, gardens ablaze with late-spring colour. Magnificent trees and shrubs – too numerous to mention – are evident, planned and planted with restraint, allowing for their full and individual appreciation, a garden of glades. Alfred Fox planted the maze in 1833, using the evergreen shrub Cherry Laurel (Prunus laurocerasus), its inspiration being the late-eighteenth-century Sydney Gardens Labyrinth in Bath.

Glendurgan is Trebah's neighbour, one of the Fox trio of original Cornish valley gardens, about 4 miles SW of Falmouth, ½ mile from Mawnan Smith. Take the route for Trebah (page 42). Glendurgan belongs to the NT, so expect a high standard of facilities, including a café. The family remains in the house and continues to contribute its expertise to the management of the 10-ha garden, nestled in what begins as three open and gentle-sided valleys that unite into a narrower and steeper-sided lower valley, which ends at the village and beach of Durgan on the Helford river. Tended by just three faithful head gardeners (1825–1960), Glendurgan was intended by its Fox founder to be 'a peace [sic] of Heaven on Earth'. Indeed it is.

Alfred Fox (1794–1874), third son of Robert Were Fox (1768–1848), came to Durgan c. 1820, renting fish cellars and orchards. Alfred ran the fishing, pilchard-salting and ex-

*Facing: The straight trunk and flat-splayed aromatic foliage of the evergreen conifer Pacific, or Western, red cedar (*Thuja plicata*). It is not a cedar at all, but belongs to the cypress family. Favoured by a number of Cornish gardens, this species was introduced into Britain by William Lobb (page 80) from his 1849–53 North American expedition. One of many different exotic tree species at Glendurgan, it can live over 1,000 years.*

port arm of the influential Fox family's business interests that included shipping, mining, copper smelting, iron and brass founding. He and his wife Sarah Lloyd (1804–90, of the Birmingham banking family) purchased the property in the 1820s and bought up leases of adjoining orchards, planting apple, cherry and abundant pear trees. In 1826 they built a thatched cottage at the head of the valley (site of the present house), renting their main residence of Wodehouse Place in Falmouth from Sir John Wodehouse in 1820 and buying it in 1868. At Glendurgan they planted shelterbelts of *Pinus pinaster*, a variety of ornamental trees and exotic shrubs such as camellias, rhododendrons and magnolias, dug the trout pond (1830) and created the laurel maze (1833). The thatched cottage was destroyed by fire in 1837 but replaced with a larger house, extended in 1891 by their son George Henry (1845–1931), a keen botanist who continued fruit growing and garden planting. He added many rhododendrons and conifers, a tradition maintained by descendants Cuthbert Lloyd (1885–1972), and Philip Hamilton (1922–2005) who jointly gave Glendurgan to the NT in 1962 – the bicentenary of the Fox family's arrival in Falmouth. Today, the family's horticultural reputation is admirably maintained here in perpetuity.

A graceful Deodar Cedar (Cedrus deodara) on the island in the Pond. This native of the western Himalayas (among Hindus it is worshipped as the 'timber of the gods') was introduced into Britain in 1831. It's a conifer – an evergreen that carries cones – with light green needles.

A giant Tulip Tree (Liriodendron tulipifera), a species first introduced to Britain from North America in 1650, and almost sure to be one of Alfred Fox's originals following their arrival at Glendurgan in the 1820s. Great gnarled branches — horizontal as well as vertical — offer both shade and shelter above the Cherry Orchard, first planted in the mid-1820s.

Gorgeously scented, creamy white flowers of the evergreen Eucryphia that flowers (each with four petals) in late summer/autumn.

Carwinion

One of the many bamboo species planted at Carwinnion.

Explorer 103: SW781283

Carwinion is one of several historic valley gardens N of the Helford river. It is open all year round, managed by the Rogers family that has lived here for over 200 years; ownership transferred to the NT in 1969. If you plan to take in other gardens related to the famous Fox family, there's bed and breakfast in the tranquil setting of Carwinion House.

Reginald Rogers (1819–77) built Carwinion and created the foundation for a 6-ha sheltered garden in the long, narrow N-S trending valley that meets the Helford river at Porth Saxon, just before the estuary meets Falmouth Bay. His son, also Reginald, developed the garden in the late-nineteenth century with his Fox cousins of Glendurgan and Trebah. There are some exceptional cedars (Tasmanian and Japanese), rhododendrons and tree ferns dating from this period, all in a delightful, unmanicured setting. Many Cornish gardens planted a wide selection of bamboo species in the 'fever' of 1890–1900, but Carwinion's comprehensive collection, many in the old walled garden and comprising over 200 varieties, dates from 1986.

Tasmanian cedar (Athrotaxis laxifolia), rare and truly exceptional, in the moist lower valley garden.

Penwarne

Explorer 103: SW773303

Penwarne, 2 miles SW of Falmouth, was the principal historic house in Mawnan, Cornwall's 'garden parish', bounded to the S by the Helford river. The present classical Georgian house was built in 1760 and commands fine views over Falmouth Bay. Its 5-ha garden, sometimes open for charity or group visits, lies at the heart of a once much larger estate – the Manor of the Penwarne family since the fourteenth century (Richard Penwarne was MP for Penryn in 1620). Sir Michael Nowell of Falmouth, merchant and adventurer of Penryn, left Penwarne to his nephew Stephen Usticke of Botallack (Sir Michael's sister, Philippa, married William Usticke in 1752), and portions were sold to become Penjerrick, Glendurgan and Trebah.

John Penwarne (1756–1836) laid the foundations for development by the Revd Michael Nowell Peters in the 1870s and by the Revd John Tonkin c. 1900. The woodland garden boasts fine specimen trees, camellias, rhododendrons and magnolias, and there are ponds fed by springs. A Victorian walled garden now hosts a swimming pool.

Tregothnan

View N from above the deer park and W edge of the botanical gardens to Tregothnan House (church of St Michael Penkevil and Tresillian river at top). The pinnacles are a characteristic signature of William Wilkins. The Pleasure Gardens are to the right, with the Drive visible. The grass and gravel parterre on the (S) Garden Front, with two long reflecting pools, was completed in 2004.

Looking NE from The Cove on the tidal Truro river to the 'House at the Head of the Valley'. Humphry Repton, who effectively succeeded Lancelot 'Capability' Brown (1715–83), designed this view (including the shelterbelts, left) when he produced his Red Book (Tregothnan's is actually blue) for the 4th Viscount (later 1st Earl) at Tregothnan in 1809. Although he advised on the house in 1811, his death meant that the enlargement of the house in the 1820s was by William Wilkins of Norfolk. The 1652 manor house was refaced, reroofed and incorporated into the new Tregothnan.

Explorer 105: SW857417

Tregothnan Estate (private) lies some 3 miles SE of Truro and less than ½ mile S of St Michael Penkevil. The Tudor-style gatehouse at Tresillian Lodge, built of yellow London Stock brick with stucco façade, bearing the Boscawen coat of arms, is a familiar landmark on the bend of the A390 (the old Truro-Grampound Turnpike of 1754) at the head of Tresillian Creek. A four-mile carriage drive leads to the grand Tudor Gothic-style mansion and Cornwall's largest historic garden, set in parkland on a wooded peninsula bounded by the River Fal and the Truro river. Tregothnan has been home to the Boscawen family, and the seat of the Viscounts Falmouth, since 1335. The house remains private, but the impressive 40-ha formal and woodland gardens open annually for their always well-attended spring charity weekends. You can also make an appointment for a private tour.

The Boscawen family has an interesting history; some highlights may explain part of the grandeur still evident at Tregothnan. They first arrived there in 1335, when John Boscawen (1317–57) of St Buryan married heiress Johanna De Tregothnan. In 1358 their son, John Boscawen (born 1336), married Joan De Albalanda (born 1338), heiress of the Manor of Blanchland, who brought with her estates in Kea and Kenwyn that, centuries later, would yield fabulous roy-

The lawn in front of the summerhouse flanked by the huge Tree Rhododendron (Rhododendron arboreum) *'Cornish Red'.*

alties from tin and copper mines. Hugh Boscawen (1578–1641) married Margaret Rolle (1600–35), from the Devonshire family of immense wealth in Petrockstowe. Their second son, Hugh (1625–1701), was a member of the Commonwealth Parliament after the Civil War (his older brother, Nicholas, was in the Parliamentary regiment of horse and was killed). Hugh abandoned the Plantagenet house that was 'sacked' by Royalists during the Civil War (its doorway remains incorporated as the kitchen garden entrance) and started to build a new house in 1650, mar-

rying Lady Margaret Clinton (eldest daughter of the 12th Baron Clinton) in 1651. Hugh Boscawen's nephew, another Hugh (1680–1734), inherited and was created Viscount Falmouth (also Baron Boscawen-Rose) in 1720 for services to George I as Controller of the Household. His son, Hugh (1706–82, 2nd Viscount) continued to reap an increasing fortune from the former Blanchland Manor across the river to the W. This comprised most of the E (Kea) side of the Carnon Valley from Bissoe to Chacewater and Scorrier, and included the major portions of rich tin and

Fruit trees in full April blossom. There have been fruit trees at Tregothnan for centuries, a reminder of the Fal's famous market gardening heritage of plums, cherries and apples.

tect William Wilkins (1778–1839), who in 1832–8 designed London's National Gallery facing the newly created Trafalgar Square. Edward Boscawen was created First Earl Falmouth in 1821. George Henry (1811–52, 2nd Earl) added to the house in 1845–8 to the designs of London architect Lewis Vulliamy (1791–1871). The Estate was inherited by a cousin, Evelyn (1819–89, 6th Viscount), a highly successful racehorse breeder and

copper mines such as Great Wheal Baddern, Nangiles and other mines that later became Wheal Jane and Mount Wellington, Creegbrawse & Penkevil, Killifreth, Hallenbeagle and Great Wheal Busy. They also owned more mines, destined to become rich in copper and tin – Botallack perhaps being the most prominent. George Evelyn (1758–1808, 3rd Viscount) succeeded his uncle, followed by his son, Edward (1787–1841). In 1809, Humphry Repton (1752–1818) was invited to advise on both house and park, Edward later rebuilding the house in 1816–18 as a picturesque Tudor castle under archi-

runner (who never bet). Evelyn was mostly responsible, in the 1850s and 1860s, for laying out the gardens, much as we know them today, ably assisted by his brother the Revd Hon. John Townshend Boscawen (1820–89), rector of Lamorran. They introduced rhododendrons from Hooker's Himalayan expedition and exotic trees and shrubs including camellias; indeed *Camellia sinensis* (tea plant) has grown at Tregothnan since Repton's days, probably the earliest camellias grown in the open in Britain. Since 2005, the Estate has supplied England's first and only tea.

Trelissick

Low aerial looking N over parkland to Trelissick House and the River Fal. The second storey of the early-nineteenth-century wings (left and right of the original house) was added by Carew Davies Gilbert, while the Solarium (right) with its central Ionic doorway, was built in the 1930s. The farm, stables and water tower can be seen (centre left) with the mid-nineteenth-century brick-walled Kitchen Garden behind the house. The garden is located mostly in the valley E of the house, sheltered by Carcaddon and North woods (higher left and right) and South Wood (centre right).

Trelissick sits high above the W bank of the River Fal, some 275 m W of King Harry Ferry and 3 miles SSE of Truro. Follow brown signs from the A39 at Carnon Downs, or take a ferry from Truro, Falmouth or St Mawes. The Estate occupies its own peninsula, jutting into the Fal before the river widens into Cornwall's largest estuary, its outer tidal basin of Carrick Roads forming one of the finest natural harbours in Europe. Trelissick's delightful 12-ha woodland garden and extensive parkland with panoramic river views belong to the NT and open to the public. A garden restaurant serves lunch or tea.

Trelesyk is recorded in 1280, its first 'modern' house dating from the mid-eighteenth century when it was built (on the site of earlier dwellings) for Captain John Lawrence of the Cornwall Militia. The mansion was

My favourite view of the house: looking N from Channals Creek, the head of which is dammed to form a lake. This view, up the gentle grassy slope from Trelissick Beach, reminds me of a smaller version of Ralph Allen's Prior Park in Bath (seen from the Palladian bridge), its six-columned Ionic portico surmounted by a pediment. Ralph Allen owned the Bath Stone (yellow Oolitic limestone) quarries from which he 'built' Bath; a wedding-gift shipment went to Thomas Daniell with which he built the Mansion House in Prince's Street, Truro.

The iconic Victorian Gothic water tower (now NT holiday accommodation) was built in 1865 as a lofty reservoir for Trelissick Mansion, its height ensuring a good head of water to fight a house fire – only too common in Victorian Cornwall.

designed by Edmund Davy of Varfell, Ludgvan, grandfather of Sir Humphry Davy, and set in a 142-ha landscaped park. On John's death in 1790, his widow let parts of the estate,

including King Harry Quay, to Ralph Allen Daniell (1762–1823), a well-known 'merchant adventurer' of Cornish mining. He was the only son of Thomas Daniell (1715–93), descended from a string of Truro mayors, and chief clerk to mining magnate William Lemon (1696–1760), who bought Carclew (pages 69–72) in 1749. Thomas bought Lemon's lucrative copper and tin mining interests in 1760 after marrying Elizabeth Elliott, niece and heiress of Cornishman Ralph Allen (1693–1764), English postal system reformer of Prior Park, Bath. Ralph Allen Daniell earned the nickname 'Guinea-a-minute' Daniell as Wheal Towan, Porthtowan, threw up so much rich copper ore from so close to surface – an occurrence that William Lemon and Thomas Daniell had experienced (1757) at Wheal Virgin, Gwennap. Under Ralph Allen Daniell, in April and May 1805 alone, Wheal Towan sold £15,200 of copper ore at a profit of £10,300! 1805 saw the Lawrence family in financial difficulty, and the sale of Trelissick to a creditor – Ralph Allen Daniell. Trelissick's new owner planted shelterbelts, but it was his son Thomas (died 1866) who, after 1825, engaged architect Peter Frederick Robinson (1776–1858) to remodel the house in Grecian style (adding the famous columned portico), much as we see it today.

Colourful mophead hydrangeas (hortensias) thrive in the damp along Hydrangea Walk above The Dell, their strong blues indicative of lime-free soil (blues turn pink on alkaline soil). Trelissick's collection was essentially established by the Copelands and continued by the NT. Over 150 different cultivars put on an annual summer-autumn spectacular.

He also added miles of rides and carriage drives, his excessive expenditure, combined with declining mining and agricultural revenues, leading to his bankruptcy in 1835. Earl Falmouth of Tregothnan, within sight of Trelissick, bought the Estate and, after unsuccessful attempts at sale (through public auction), sold it in 1844 to John Davies Gilbert (1811–54), son of distinguished Cornish engineer and author Davies Giddy (changed to Gilbert in 1818), a High Sheriff of Cornwall. John, and later his son Carew Davies Gilbert (1852–1913), continued planting the parkland, established orchards and intro-

duced many exotic plants into the garden. Merchant banker Leonard Cunliffe (a former Governor of the Bank of England) bought the Estate from Gilbert's executors in 1913 and, in 1937, it passed to his stepdaughter Ida Copeland (1876–1964). Her husband was Ronald Copeland (1884–1958), president and chairman of Spode-Copeland, Staffordshire bone china manufacturers and potters to the Royal family since 1806. They gifted Trelissick to the NT in 1955, and in 2013 Ronald and Ida's grandson vacated the house. The NT secured many items and hopes to open the house in some capacity in 2014.

Enys

Explorer 105: SW792364

The 400-ha Enys Estate is a little over 1 mile NNE of Penryn, adjacent to Mylor Bridge in the E and a longstanding neighbour to Carclew in the N. The Estate lodge, alongside the road N from St Gluvias, heralds a ²/₃-mile-long carriage drive. This leads NE through former parkland – with great clumps of old, 12-m-high 'Cornish Red' underplanting shelterbelt – passing into arboretum and shrubbery before eventually reaching the house. The Estate has been owned by the same family since 1272 but the gardens, little known, long neglected and now being rescued and conserved, have been in the care

Facing: Looking W to Enys House along the margin between the former gardens and park (left). The mansion (top left) was rebuilt in the 1830s; its service wing (adjoining to the right) is eighteenth-century; the coach house and stables (top centre) are 1840s. The structure of the garden and grounds is much earlier. Many original features survive and are especially clear from the air: one of two pyramidal roofed pavilions (bottom right) can be seen in the Walled Garden (lower right quadrant); remnants of the Italianate garden depicted by Borlase, and the furthest extent of the gardens at that time; the ancient Ponds in the valley of the Enys Brook (top right).

Overleaf: May carpet of bluebells in Parc Lye, believed to be undisturbed since medieval times.

Sinuous edges of the Ponds (three in total), cut in the 1830s from two formal, mid-eighteenth-century, straight-sided canals (connected by a cascade), resembling the Elizabethan fishponds on the same site. Candelabra primulas line the banks of the planned walk, still used today. Clumps of feathery bamboo (Enys has a fine collection, including a number of rare varieties) are a reminder of the New Zealand garden established by JD Enys who, after the death of his younger brother and at the request of his mother, returned in 1891 after 30 years in New Zealand. He inherited Enys in 1906 on his older brother's death.

of the Enys Trust since 2002. (John Davies Enys [1837–1912] catalogued the plants at Enys in 1909, and this list is referred to in restocking the garden.) They are open on certain days from April to September, and in bluebell season put on an unparalleled show.

Enys (= tongue of land) probably refers to the peninsula bounded by Penryn and Mylor creeks. Robert de Enys lived here in the time of Edward I, establishing a family seat that lasted over 600 years. After the Elizabethan era, formal structure came under Samuel Enys (1611–97), a successful merchant and MP for Penryn. He married Elizabeth Pendarves, whose family was enriched through buying Glasney land after the Reformation. The 'fine gardens' at Enys, under another Samuel (1681–1744), were the first in Cornwall cited for their beauty in a published volume – Camden's *Britannia*. Family members married well, had shrewd business acumen and invested wisely, particularly in Cornish mines as mineral lords and adventurers, owning land in almost 30 parishes. The eighteenth century (and much of the nineteenth) saw large revenues from tin and copper mining, including mines in Perranzabuloe, Kea, Kenwyn, Camborne, Wendron and St Agnes. In the early eighteenth century, for example, the Tonkins' Manor of Trevaunance was repossessed by Samuel Enys, including the rich Wheal Trevaunance. The family had extensive interests in merchant supplies to mines, and in tin smelting at Calenick. Sustained cashflow enabled repeated enhancement of the house and estate. The enrichment of the garden, particularly in terms of species, came via plant collector and avid geologist JD Enys. Many of his introductions can still be seen.

Carclew

Central section of the S, entrance, front of Carclew Mansion, the most dramatic elevation of extensive ruins set in shelterbelt first planted in the early nineteenth century. The impressive tetra-style portico, constructed in Cornish granite like the rest of the house, is in the Ionic order and marks the entrance hall in grand classical style. The house was begun by Samuel Kempe in the 1720s, and completed in the 1750s by architect Thomas Edwards under direction of its new owner, mining magnate William Lemon, who bought the estate in 1749. The mansion was gutted by fire in 1934.

The romantic Palladian ruins of Carclew Mansion stand tall above the undergrowth on commanding heights above Restronguet Creek. Less than 1 mile (as the crow flies) SSW of Devoran, and 1 mile from the A39 Falmouth Road as it passes alongside Perran Creek and through the Kennall Valley, they are strictly private, but part of the garden is open for limited charity days in the spring. Carclew Estate once contained one of the finest eighteenth-century houses in Cornwall, exceptional formal terraced and water gardens, and was occupied by what is now one of the lesser-known but nonetheless great Cornish dynasties: the Lemon family.

Carclew (Cargelew in the twelfth century) was once owned by the Bonython family, an only child and heiress, Jane (1681–1749), marrying the Penryn merchant Samuel Kempe (1669–1728). On her death, Carclew was left to her cousin James Bonython of Creed, who sold it for £3,300 to 'the Great Mr Lemon' (1696–1760) of Truro (Lemon Street and Lemon Quay remember the great William Lemon). William was born in Germoe, and started working life as a humble tinner. He soon landed a responsible position as a clerk to Bristol copper smelter John Coster (1647–1718) and his sons, who did much to initiate deep copper mining in Cornwall. He founded the family fortune after marriage to wealthy Isabella Vibert of Gulval in 1721, followed by sustained investment in copper mining, first at Wheal Fortune, Ludgvan, where he had already adventured with Blewett & Dewen of Marazion, employing a Newcomen engine which was pumping the mine by 1720. Wheal Fortune lived up to its name, enabling Lemon to invest in new copper quays in Hayle and to move to Truro, where he was elected Mayor in 1737 and appointed Sheriff in 1742. For the rest of his life William enhanced his considerable fortune – in spectacular fashion – taking leases of mines in Gwennap – soon dubbed Cornwall's 'Copper Kingdom'. Mines in which he 'adventured' – and employed the latest steam-engine pumping technology – included such prolific producers as Wheal Unity (the Lemon family's quarter-share netted over £50,000 in dividends) and Poldice, where he was principal adventurer, with John Williams I (1685–1761) of Burncoose as Manager. Lemon also invested in tin smelting and bought numerous estates and property. He engaged Thomas Edwards of Greenwich to enlarge and complete Kempe's unfinished

Carclew grounds, now in divided ownership but still retaining much historic structure and significant exotic planting: the rectangular eighteenth-century Higher and Lower Ponds (centre to top left, surrounded by rhododendron and azalea), late-eighteenth/early-nineteenth-century terraced walled gardens on four levels (lower left), and fine, *brick-built, late-eighteenth-century coach house and stables (lower right). Magnificent woodland (top) rises towards the former mansion and contains original planting, including mature Lucombe oaks (William Lucombe worked here) and Lobb's sequoias.*

house at Carclew. (In 1737, Edwards had been architect of Princes House, Lemon's Truro town house.)

William's son, William Junior (1725–57), predeceased his father, so all estates were left in trust to grandson, Sir William (1748–1824).

At this time, Thomas Daniell (1715–93) of Truro, former chief clerk to William Lemon and a trustee to his estates, acquired copper-mining interests that later made the Daniells famously wealthy. Sir William continued in his grandfather's tradition, leasing new copper mines during the 1760s–80s, in particular from the Beauchamps of Pengreep, where setts taken included those that amalgamated in the 1780s to become the fabulous United Mines, from which Lemon (and co-adventurers such as the Foxes) extracted a profit of no less than £300,000 before 1800. In the late-eighteenth/early-nineteenth century, Sir William poured cash into Carclew, extending the mansion and embellishing the garden and grounds. His daughters married well, including Caroline to John Hearle Tremayne (1780–1851) of Heligan (pages 112–19) in 1818, and Harriet to Francis Basset (1st Baron de Dunstanville) of Tehidy (pages 86–8) in 1824; their gardens (as well as their business interests) benefitted from close association with Carclew in the years to come. On Sir William's death, Carclew and all 'Lemon mines' passed to the third son, Sir Charles, 2nd Baronet (1784–1868).

Charles Lemon was one of Cornwall's leading horticulturists, aided by talented Head Gardener William Booth, a camel-lia expert (the Lobb brothers worked here too, before they left for Veitch of Exeter). Charles founded the Royal Horticultural Society of Cornwall in 1832, and Carclew became a hotbed of new plant introductions, many sourced from local sea captains. Within a decade, Nepalese rhododendron was in full bloom at Carclew, from seed planted as early as 1822 – a genus for which this Cornish garden became synonymous. Sir William Hooker (1785–1865, Director of Kew) was a close friend, and Charles was a key sponsor of his plant-hunting son, Joseph (1817–1911), returning 43 new species of rhododendron from Sikkim and Nepal (1847–51) – and *Magnolia campbellii*, the herald of Cornish spring.

Sir Charles suffered successive family tragedies – including the losses of his wife, Charlotte, and three children. He never re-married and, as he had no surviving children, the baronetcy became extinct on his death in 1868. Carclew passed to a nephew, Colonel Arthur Tremayne (1827–1905) of Heligan, who took up residence at Carclew. Much of the property was sold in 1920 and the mansion was tragically gutted by fire in 1934.

Burncoose

The woodland garden at Burncoose contains well-labelled exotics such as this Rhododendron campylocarpum, one of the finest yellow-flowering species sent back by Hooker in 1849 from his Sikkim-Himalayas expedition. Many plants seen in the garden may be purchased from the sales area in the walled gardens near the entrance.

Explorer 104: SW743391

Burncoose, the well-known nursery and woodland garden, lies less than 1 mile SSE of Gwennap church, close to the A393 Redruth-Falmouth road. It is open all year

Facing: Camellia x williamsii *JC Williams. Camellias are associated especially with the Williams family, in particular 'JC' of Caerhays who did much to promote them in British gardens by creating the* williamsii *hybrids in the 1920s (at first crossing the pink-flowered* Camellia saluenensis, *brought back by Forrest, with a red-flowered* Camellia japonica.) *Hardy and abundantly flowering, many have since been bred and raised at Burncoose.*

Above: View to the entrance front of Burncoose House, site of the first home built (1715) by the Williams mining dynasty in this favourable, S-facing setting, close to the mines which the family managed. This house is mostly early-nineteenth-century (with mid-nineteenth-century additions), when the family controlled a major percentage of Cornish mines and were bankers, holding dominant positions in the lucrative trades of tin smelting in Cornwall and copper smelting in Swansea.

Camellia 'Donation' at Burncoose.

(1753–1841), who built and planted Scorrier in 1778, eventually leaving Burncoose to one of his sons, John III (1777–1849). In 1809 the Williamses collaborated with the Foxes in the construction of the Portreath Tramroad, in 1813 with the Foxes and brother-in-law Collan Harvey of St Day in a partnership for developing Portreath Harbour, and in 1814 (with the addition of Stephen Davey) in the establishment of Portreath Tin Smelting House. In 1822, the Welsh copper smelting partnership of Fox, Williams, Grenfell & Co. (later Williams, Foster & Co.) was formed, and in 1837 the tin smelting partnership of Williams, Harvey & Co. (with Richard Harvey, 1808–70) that came to dominate Cornish tin smelting. Under John III, the house was extended in the early nineteenth century and the garden developed. On his death, a nephew, John Michael (1813–89), inherited and further improved Burncoose. The 12-ha woodland garden we see today, however, began largely as a late-nineteenth-century/early-twentieth-century creation, mostly by Mrs Charlotte Rogers, second daughter of John Michael Williams (1813–80) of Caerhays (pages 106–111), from where many fine plants were introduced.

but the house, remaining in the Williams family, is strictly private.

Burncoose is first recorded in 1277 as Burncoys (derived from Cornish for wooded hill). In 1715, John Williams I (1685–1761) acquired the estate and built a house, thus establishing the family in the Gwennap Mining District. John I later became mining agent to William Lemon and commenced one of the greatest mining engineering feats in Cornwall – the Great County Adit.

John's son, Michael I (1730–75), inherited, to be succeeded by his son, John II

Scorrier

View N over parkland and 2-ha woodland garden to Scorrier House (centre), St Agnes Beacon and the Celtic Sea beyond. Rich copper and tin mines once surrounded the Scorrier Estate, and the Portreath Tramroad – started in 1809 by the Williamses and Foxes to transport copper ore and coal to and from their harbour at Portreath – passed along its E boundary. The surrounding countryside is rich in industrial archaeology: in addition to the mines and mineral tramways, mining villages and Methodist chapels, Scorrier House – and other country houses closely associated with the mining industry – form a key part of the Cornish Mining World Heritage Site.

View to the N entrance front of Scorrier House and its distinctive arched porte-cochère *with pyramidal glazed roof. In 1778, John Williams II built a house and planted the grounds at Scorrier; part of the L-shaped service wing (higher centre left) is eighteenth-century, as are the E lawn terrace and 90-m granite ha-ha (centre far left). In 1845, Michael Williams II substantially enlarged the house, adding the stately E front that still overlooks the park. George Williams (1827–90) inherited from his father, and in 1862 had to rebuild parts of the house after a fire. In February 1908 Scorrier suffered another fire, and the H-shaped main house was largely gutted. Restored in the same year, new fire precautions included the introduction of teak and concrete, including a low-hipped concealed roof.*

Explorer 104: SW725438

Scorrier, 2 miles NE of Redruth, is the historic seat of the 'mining' Williams family. Seven generations have resided here, and the 182-ha oasis of parkland and garden – with links to famous Cornish plant hunter William Lobb

– remains the setting for their private family home. Increasingly the property, only 730 m from the A30, is used for wedding receptions and even as a film set. The garden is open by appointment and for spring charity events.

By 1778, when John Williams II (1753–1841) built Scorrier, he was agent for no less than 22 local mines. In 1805 he was seeking to acquire a copper works in Swansea, in 1806 purchased Calstock Manor (for its silver, copper and tin prospects), in 1809 started the Poldice Tramroad, and in 1813 formed a partnership (with Fox and Harvey) for improving Portreath Harbour. The Williams family was also running the two greatest copper mines in Cornwall: Consolidated and United in Gwennap. They went on to multiply their fortune by engaging in lucrative Swansea copper smelting (and the corresponding metal market in London), taking over the Morfa Copper Works in 1831 that became the largest non-ferrous metal smelter in the world. They engaged in banking (the Cornish Bank and the West Cornwall Bank) and, from 1837, their tin-smelting portfolio mushroomed as the soon to be pre-eminent Williams, Harvey & Company.

John II retired to Sandhill House, Gunnislake (pages 150–51), in 1832 (after remarrying, to a young bride, a Miss Edwards aged

Quartz crystals (top) and green fluorite, once a common associate of copper ores in Gwennap. In the garden at Scorrier a nineteenth-century planting of camellias (some of the earliest Japanese camellias planted out of doors in Britain) leads to the Quartz Grotto, a reminder of the family's mining past, and of the internationally renowned mineral collection assembled in the house. Started by John II c. 1780, and continued by successive generations until the 1880s, there were once in excess of 14,000 specimens. In 1863 the collection was moved to Caerhays, and in 1891 and 1893 it was divided and mostly donated to several institutions; a choice selection remaining at Caerhays.

25), his son Michael Williams II (1785–1858) taking on Scorrier. Michael bought Caerhays in 1854, breaking away from his family's 140 years of living beside 'the richest square mile in the Old World'. But the Williamses continued to live there, as they do today.

The garden at Scorrier is most famously associated with the Cornish plant hunter William Lobb (1809–64), not least for its Champion Monkey Puzzle. William, and his brother Thomas (1811–94), the other famous plant hunter, came from a family who lived on the Pencarrow estate (pages 133–6) at Washaway, where their father was a carpenter. They began their horticultural trajectory at Carclew (pages 69–72), under Sir Charles Lemon, before gaining employment with James Veitch (1792–1863) who established a nursery at Mount Radford in Exeter in 1832. In 1837, both brothers were working for Veitch at Killerton, but in the same year William was sent on a three-year horticultural secondment to Stephen Davey (1785–1864) of Redruth. Stephen (and his brother Richard) was in the same mining managerial mould as the Williamses, and partnered them in many ventures (their father, William Davey, was a lawyer and had been manager of Consolidated Mines in Gwennap in 1819). So it is no surprise that

William worked in the gardens at Scorrier (two of Stephen's daughters later married into the Williams family: Elizabeth to John Michael of Burncoose in 1852, and Charlotte to George of Scorrier in 1859).

In 1840, William Lobb left Redruth for some herbarium training at Kew before returning to embark on HM packet *Seagull* (a schooner, 279 tons) at Falmouth, bound for Rio de Janeiro. On arrival in Brazil, William's gift to the young Dom Pedro II (1825–91), second and last ruler of the Empire of Brazil, was some seeds of the rhododendron hybrid 'Cornish Red', duly planted in the gardens of the Imperial Palace at Petropolis. While collecting for Veitch in Chile, Lobb also quietly despatched seeds of the 'Chile Pine' (later 'Monkey Puzzle') to his old employer at Scorrier, where they took pride of place in the pinetum. Here too, the South American conifer Prince Albert's Yew (*Saxegothaea conspicua*) survives from Lobb's original seed.

Tregullow

View SW to Tregullow House, 365 m SE of Scorrier House (centre right) and set in the same swathe of Williams family parkland less than 2 miles from Redruth (Carn Brea, top left). The classical house in white-painted stucco – much reduced in size after the First World War – was built in 1826 for William Williams. The woodland garden, like its neighbour Scorrier, is associated with Cornish plant hunter William Lobb (pages 80, 82). Fine specimen trees and the spring colour of rhododendron create an arc beside and behind the house; the entrance front, with rectangular tetrastyle porte-cochère, overlooks the lawn that leads to a belt of woodland flanking the B3298 road from Scorrier to Carharrack. A delightful Victorian conservatory is attached to the left return wall.

Tregullow, a prominent seat of the 'mining' Williamses, was built in 1826 for William Williams (1791–1870). It was sited within 57 ha of former common enclosed and planted by his father, John Williams II (1753–1841), who built Scorrier House (pages 77–80) in 1778. William became High Sheriff of Cornwall in 1851, and was created 1st Baronet Williams of Tregullow in 1866 (the house, once considerably larger, contained service quarters for 13 female and 3 male servants at that time).

Sir William was the third and last surviving son of John and Catherine (née Harvey), and at the time of his death was Deputy-Lieutenant and magistrate for Cornwall, a deputy-warden of the Stannaries, and chairman of the East Kerrier Highway Board. He had retired from partnership in the well-known copper company of Williams, Foster & Co. (in 1862) but remained senior partner in the firms of Williams, Harvey & Co. (tin smelters, Truro), Williams's Portreath Co. (coal merchants, Portreath), and Williams's Perran Foundry Co. (founders and engine-makers, Perran-ar-worthal). He was a partner in the Cornish Bank at Truro, Redruth, Falmouth and Penryn, and in the firm of Williams & Sons (Scorrier). As a mining adventurer he was justly celebrated, having large interests in sulphur mines in Wicklow, lead mines in Wales, and in the mines of his native Gwennap district in Cornwall. Moreover, he held three-quarters of the Clifford Amalgamated Mines in Gwennap, and the greater share of Dolcoath in Illogan. He also held a large portion of the Cook's Kitchen, Carn Brea, South Crofty, and West Basset interests.

The garden at Tregullow benefitted from many early introductions by Cornish plant hunter William Lobb (1809–64). He worked for Veitch of Exeter and, prior to his plant-hunting expeditions that began in 1840, had been sent by Veitch to assist the horticultural enterprise of the wealthy Stephen Davey (1785–1864) of Redruth. Davey was manager of various mines owned by Williams and, after gardening at Scorrier and no doubt Tregullow, seeds were sent back from Lobb's expeditions to South America (1840–44 and 1845–8) and California (1849–53, and 1854–8). Lobb, like so many Cornish compatriots, was in California during much of the California Gold Rush (1848–55), but remained loyal to his passion for botanical work. When his contract with Veitch expired in 1858, he remained in this new American state (California only came under American control in 1847) until his death in 1864.

Pengreep

Pengreep House was built in the early eighteenth century for the wealthy Beauchamp family who were extensively involved in mining affairs. It was enlarged in the mid-eighteenth century, and again in 1865, latterly for John Michael Williams who also owned Caerhays. Below the carriage ring, with central sundial, the lawn meets ornamental lakes that are connected by cascades and bordered by walks. There was once a strange custom of children taking their dolls to be christened at Pengreep on Good Friday.

Rhododendron coming into bloom in the linear, rectangular, formal garden that is aligned with the long axis of the house (to its NE side), parallel with the service drive.

Explorer 104: SW747387

Pengreep is a strictly private estate in a sheltered, wooded valley immediately SE of Burncoose, Gwennap. Burncoose (pages 73–6) is connected historically through the marriage of Elizabeth Beauchamp of Pengreep to Michael Williams of Burncoose.

The Beauchamp family (originally, since the twelfth century, from Binnerton, Crowan) became the principal landowner in Gwennap in 1550 when Martin Beauchamp married Margaret, daughter and heir to Henry Trefyns of Trefyns (Trevince [page 85]). The Beauchamps moved their seat to Pengreep in the early eighteenth century, the family growing increasingly wealthy from mineral royalties, especially from copper. The represented Cornwall with High Sheriffs in 1755 (Francis) and 1784 (Joseph). Lucrative mining leases (setts) were granted to William Lemon, and later Sir William Lemon, of Carclew (pages 69–72), with the Williams family as managers. This successful operational equation included mines at Poldice (from the 1750s) and on Cusgarne Downs (from the 1750s–80s onwards), which concealed one of Cornwall's longest and most productive copper lodes that was eventually exploited by the legendary United Mines. Merchant Collan Harvey (1770–1846), partner in many mining ventures with the Williams family (John Williams of Scorrier married Catherine Harvey, Collan's sister, in 1776), retired to Pengreep on the £350,000 he received for his share of the business that included Portreath Harbour, Williams Harvey tin smelters and Williams, Foster & Co., copper smelters in Swansea. After his death, at Pengreep, John Michael Williams (1830–80, who also inherited an uninhabitable Caerhays Castle [pages 106–11] in 1858) moved here, extended the mansion in 1865, and then leased it in 1876 to the Ford family (related by marriage to the Beauchamps).

Trevince

The private estate of Trevince is an ancient one, Robert de Trefyns being recorded as lord of the manor in 1281. Margaret, daughter and heir to Henry Trefyns of Trefyns (Trevince) married Martin Beauchamp in 1550 and built an Elizabethan manor house 275 m to the NW of the church of St Weneppa (founded on a Celtic monastery and today the site of Gwennap's seventeenth-century parish church). During the eighteenth century, the Beauchamps transferred to Pengreep (pages 83–4) and Trevince was leased to Michael Williams (1730–75) and his wife Susanna (1732–1814), only daughter of

Trevince, from above Gwennap Church.

John Beauchamp of Trevince. Michael Williams (1785–1858, second son of John Williams II of Scorrier) considerably improved the property and remained here until his death. It was substantially extended to the W (left) in the 1870s when the entrance front, with its distinctive canted three-window bay facing S, was built at right angles to the main eastern range with its adjoining farmhouse (right). Trevince remains in the ownership of descendants of the Beauchamps. (David Cameron, who became Prime Minister in 2010, is also said to be a descendant.)

Tehidy

Explorer 104: SW647434

Tehidy Country Park, 2 miles N of Camborne and less than 1 mile from North Cliffs, is nestled in the largest single area of woodland in west Cornwall. A convenient access is via South Lodge, one of two original thatched *cottages ornées*, dating from 1792. It opens off Mount Whistle Road on to South Drive that heads N into the Old Park and turns W into a public car-park – before reaching Tehidy Golf Course (once the deer park). Owned by Cornwall Council since 1983, the park is a treasured community recreation facility with over 9 miles of winding woodland paths. There are ducks and swans, and a good show of bluebells each year. Despite the destruction of the Mansion by fire in 1919, and the terminal decline of the formal gardens that began during the First World War, there is still a great sense of history in the now 'wild' estate.

The Manor was ruled by the Bassets, who obtained it *c.* 1150 by marriage to an heiress of the de Dunstanvilles, whose lineage is linked to Reginald de Dunstanville (1110–75), Earl of Cornwall. The Basset estates were enriched through vast mining revenues from the Pool, Dolcoath and Basset mines in the eighteenth and nineteenth centuries. Pool Adit returned a fortune from shallow copper in the eighteenth century, so too Dolcoath, which then went on to become Cornwall's greatest tin mine (finally closing in 1921). A memorial to Sir Francis Basset (1757–1835), 1st Baron de Dunstanville and Basset, crowns Carn Brea; when he died, 20,000 people followed his funeral procession. In the early 1860s, when John Francis Basset (1831–69) rebuilt Tehidy, he was receiving royalties of over £20,000 per annum from Dolcoath Mine and South Wheal Frances alone. The family owned Tehidy until the early twentieth century.

The Bassets themselves left Tehidy in 1915; the Manor was sold in November 1916, and by the time of the fire the site had already become an isolation hospital for tuberculosis sufferers. The long building with portico and clock tower, between the two angle pavilions on the original E entrance front, infilled a courtyard and used pillars and masonry salvaged after the fire. It was completed by Janu-

Aerial view SW to the relict landscape of the Bassets of Tehidy. The site of the former Palladian mansion by Edwards, altered in 1861–3 by William Burn (1789–1870) of Piccadilly, is marked by the sunken garden (centre right) that utilizes its former basement. The house, described as the first 'modern' building in Cornwall, cost a staggering £150,000 and was built for John Francis Basset (1831–69), a grand-nephew of Sir Francis; he became one of the richest commoners in England when he succeeded to the estates on the death of Lady Frances Basset (1781–1855).

The house was destroyed by fire on 25 February 1919. Elements survive from an earlier (1734–9) mansion built to the design of Thomas Edwards (died 1775) of Greenwich (his first work in Cornwall) for John Pendarves Basset (1714–39). Three out of four quadrant pavilions, each with cupola and clock, surround its central site.

The Cascades in the (now 'wild') New Park designed as part of Thomas Edwards' architectural and landscape package, begun in 1734. William Harry, Estate mason, built this charming series of shallow waterfalls in 1738 from dressed Carn Brea granite 'moorstone'. They are formed in the leat-like outlet to the Lake, a 122-m-long 'sheet of water' created by excavating an already marshy area in the shallow valley S of the mansion ('Pond Field' of 1737). Here a stream, whose source is beyond Merrose Moor towards Pool, takes an E-W course before joining the Red river below Coombe on its course to Godrevy.

ary 1922. Tehidy Hospital closed in 1986, and today the buildings comprise private luxury apartments built in the mid-1990s. The lake (top left in the photo, page 87) is 180 m downslope of what would have been the garden front of the earlier mansion.

Killiow

View to the SW entrance front of Killiow House (with 1850 Doric porte-cochère, left) and early-nineteenth-century garden front with central bow. Coach house and stables behind.

Explorer 104: SW803422

Killiow occupies a SE-facing ridge, 2 miles SW of Truro and ½ mile NW of Playing Place, just off the A39 that parallels the Old Coach Road. Kea church, ½ mile to the NE, adjoins the estate. Surrounded by specimen trees and old rhododendrons, the eighteenth/nineteenth-century granite mansion (remodelled in 1850) is a private residence, though the Killiow Golf Course occupies its former parkland. Daubuz's coach house (top left in the photo on page 89), and stables that surround a courtyard, is adjacent to the Home Farm and has been converted to residential apartments.

The estate was the seat of the Killiow family from the thirteenth century, and passed to successive heirs in the families of Vivian and Haweis (from the late-sixteenth century until the late-eighteenth century). In 1785, Robert Lovell Gwatkin (1757–1843), who earlier had married Theophila Palmer (1757–1848, a niece and co-heiress of Sir Joshua Reynolds), bought Killiow and extensively remodeled the house, gardens and grounds; the 'crinkle-crankle' kitchen garden wall is attributed to him also.

In 1845, William Daubuz purchased the estate; the Daubuz family (originally D'Aubus, Huguenots, who in 1685 escaped persecution in France under Louis XV) became tin smelters and mines' adventurers, established by Theophilus Daubuz (1713–74) who came to Falmouth in 1730. Lewis Charles Daubuz (1754–1839), whose son married an Arundel daughter of Kenegie, followed in his father's footsteps. William, who was High Sheriff of Cornwall in 1850, developed plantations at Killiow and introduced exotic conifers, together with Kew rhododendron seedlings grown from Joseph Hooker's original seed from his 1847–51 Himalayan expeditions.

William's son, the Revd John Daubuz, inherited in 1854 but was more interested in the Kea tradition of market gardening, and planted local varieties of plum, cherry, pear and apple. His son, John Claude Daubuz, who also inherited the Carvedras tin smelting business, continued the garden, adding more exotics, including tree ferns from Treseders in the 1890s.

John Garland Treseder (1841–1923) and his two brothers left their father's Truro nursery in 1857 to join the Victoria gold rush in Australia. John gave up the diggings and returned to Cornwall, but by the late-1870s he was back in Sydney pursuing his love of plants. He wrote directly to a number of Cornwall's great garden owners, recommending native plants that thrived in parts of what is now New South Wales, which had a similar climate to Cornwall. By 1892 he had secured orders from JC Daubuz (Killiow), Anna Maria Fox (Penjerrick), JC Williams (Caerhays), and Jonathan Rashleigh (Menabilly), among others.

Trewithen

A delightful view of Trewithen: early morning in the waning days of winter, when the delicate, lichen-clad Pentewan stone on the S front of the old mansion retains a pinkish hue from the night's moisture, and the early blooms of magnolia and arboreal rhododendron herald another Cornish spring. Flanking the scalloped 182-m-long S Lawn (Johnstone's 'great glade'), the Champion (20-m-high) Magnolia campbellii subsp. mollicomata (left) is a Chinese introduction by plant hunter George Forrest, while the Rhododendron arboreum (dominant parent of the 'Cornish Red', right) is one of 100 such hybrids planted within a year of George Johnstone's arrival in 1904.

Trewithen (= the house in the spinney) lies in Probus parish, mid-way between Truro and St Austell. The private country estate, owned by nearly ten generations of the same family since 1715, is host to one of Cornwall's 'great gardens'. The entrance to this 11-ha plantsman's paradise (predominantly a twentieth-century woodland garden) is off the A390, 320 m E of Probus roundabout. It

Facing: View S to the entrance front of Trewithen House with its recessed centre, forward flanking bays and hipped and dormered roof. Three sides of the house are built in Pentewan stone (from Pentewan Quarry owned by Hawkins), but in the late-1730s the entrance front was faced with bricks made from clay dug on site. Following the Second World War, after centuries of weathering and due to an inevitable increase in water absorption by the brickwork, this N façade was rendered to match the rest of the natural masonry. A carriage ring dominates the entrance courtyard, and either side are distinctive, mid-eighteenth-century French Pavilions, rectangular in plan, brick-built and surmounted by cupolas. The E pavilion (left, behind trees) was the coach house and stables while the W (lower right) was a brew house and laundry, both connected by curving walls to the main house, reflecting the original plan by James Gibbs. To the right of the house can be seen the eighteenth-century walled garden (originally a herb garden), 500 square metres of formality in Trewithen's otherwise gloriously informal gardens.

has all the facilities one would expect, including a teashop and a nursery with an excellent reputation. Owned by Michael Galsworthy (grandson of garden-maker George Johnstone), who came to live here with his family in 1980, the garden open season is supplemented by house openings – a rare chance to see one of Cornwall's finest eighteenth-century mansions.

Trewithen (*Trefitent*, owned by the Count of Mortain) is first mentioned in the Domesday Book of 1086, but it was the Hawkins family that was to dominate the affairs of Trewithen for nearly 200 years. They arrived in Cornwall in 1554 when John Hawkins moved to Trewinnard in St Erth. Philip Hawkins (died 1737), a wealthy barrister, bought Trewithen estate in 1715, soon extending the E-facing house and improving the garden. He commissioned James Gibbs (1682–1754), one of Britain's most influential architects who helped to formulate 'Georgian' design, to draw up some proposals. It was Gibbs who conceived the N-facing house flanked by two brick-built French Pavilions. Though title passed to Philip's son, another Philip (1700–38), building work continued through the 1730s under the supervision of London architect Thomas Edwards (died 1775). On Philip's death the estate passed to the care

Camellia Walk in winter flower at Trewithen. These stalwarts of Cornish gardens were first grown out-of-doors in Cornwall in the early nineteenth century, when their introduction accelerated with the flourishing Chinese tea trade of the East India Company (Camellia sinensis is the tea plant). They can grow over 9 m high in century-old maturity. Well-known Trewithen hybrids include 'Elizabeth Johnstone', 'Trewithen Pink', and 'Glenn's Orbit' (commemorating the American astronaut and now in the White House garden).

spent time as a boy at his uncle's house, married Anne Heywood, daughter of a wealthy London banker and cloth merchant. They came to live at Trewithen in the early 1750s. Thomas was elected to Parliament, gaining his seat in the Commons via the 'rotten borough' of Grampound, and also became a J.P. Progress under Edwards was slow, his services seemingly ending in 1761. Thomas then engaged Sir Robert Taylor (1714–88), London sculptor turned architect, for the interior design, and Matthew Brettingham for the exterior. It was Taylor's scheme that was funded while Brettingham's was either rejected or shelved. The gardens were landscaped, and Thomas was responsible for major planting – both English and 'foreign' plants – and for creating fine vistas from the house. He sadly died from a smallpox inoculation (ironically it was intended as an example to encourage his tenants), the estate then passing to his eldest surviving son, Christopher (1758–1829), while he was still a minor.

Christopher trained as a lawyer, and in 1791 was made a baronet for public services and loyalty to Prime Minister William Pitt (the Younger). Sir Christopher did much to sustain and enhance the family wealth, and never married. With his substantial inheritance he bought several nearby Cornish estates that

of his sister, Mary (1694–1780), and her husband, Christopher (1694–1767), who lived at Trewinnard but managed the building works until their son, Thomas Hawkins (1724–66), came of age. Thomas, who had

Rhododendron macabeanum, one of Trewithen's most famous plantings from seed collected by Kingdon-Ward in 1928. George Johnstone had offered Lt.-Col. Edward Bolitho of Trengwainton a share in Kingdon-Ward's 1927–8 plant-hunting expedition to Assam and the Mishmi Hills in Upper Burma. The friends shared seed from the collection, the species first flowering at Trengwainton, though it takes 60 years for the plants to reach maturity. When he first saw it at an elevation of nearly 3,000 m in the E Himalayas (Japvo Peak near Kohima, India), Kingdon-Ward recorded that it 'bears huge trusses of lemon-yellow flowers, stained plum-juice purple at the base.'

included lands rich in silver-lead (and, elsewhere, china clay). Two such acquisitions, both in 1798, were the ancient manors of Cargol, that Philip had once leased, and Treludra (Newlyn East and Mitchell). After instigating deep ploughing at Shepherds, for the purpose of folding sheep (hence the place-name), an outcrop of a rich silver-lead lode (vein) was discovered when the plough threw up rich stones of galena. Hawkins worked the Old Shepherds Mine, profitably and on his own account (as mineral owner and 'adventurer'), laying out £5,000 per year on wages. Wheal Rose followed in 1814 (in 1820 a silver block worth £1,500 was smelted here), and in 1823 the mine was let by Hawkins (as lord) to Stephen Davey of Redruth, who paid Hawkins £6,544 in dues between 1824 and 1831. Further discoveries on Hawkins' land included, in 1834, the celebrated East Wheal Rose. This mine became the richest lead producer in Cornwall, and by 1846 employed over 1,200 men, women and children; the same year, a sustained downpour flooded the valley where the main shafts lay, drowning 39 miners in Cornwall's worst mining disaster. Between 1818 and 1826 Sir Christopher Hawkins rebuilt Pentewan harbour (its first construction, in 1744, was by the Hawkins estate), making Pentewan into a china clay port. In 1829 he built a four-mile, horse-drawn tramway that linked the port to china clay pits on his land at St Austell; in 1886 a steam locomotive that arrived on the line was named 'Trewithen'.

On Christopher's death his brother, John Hawkins (1761–1841, of Bignor Park, Sussex), looked after Trewithen and spent time between estates planting many fine trees; he died at Trewithen in 1841. Title had passed to his son, Christopher Henry Thomas Hawkins (1820–1903), in 1829. 'CHT' chose not to live in Cornwall, but his widow made a significant contribution to the building of Truro Cathedral.

Trewithen, and Bignor Park, passed to nephew John Johnstone (1850–1904) who, dying a year later, left these great estates to his son, George Johnstone (1882–1960). George began to clear and plant a new garden of 'excitement and discovery' within the eighteenth-century framework. He received advice from JC Williams of Caerhays and sponsored plant-hunting expeditions by EH Wilson (1876–1930), George Forrest (1873–1932) and Frank Kingdon-Ward (1885–1958). During the First World War the government requisitioned 300 beech trees (British and Canadian troops received them along the Western Front as trench-props), and this resulted in George's masterpiece of the Great Glade or South Lawn. With the continued help of his dear friend 'JC', and the expertise of his head gardener, Jack Skilton, George was lucky enough to see many of his splendid introductions reach maturity. For us, too, it is fortunate that subsequent family members have shared George's passion, Trewithen remaining a truly 'great garden'.

Trerice

The Dutch-style (scroll-gabled) entrance front to the charming Elizabethan manor house built for the wealthy Sir John Arundell (father-in-law to Sir Richard Carew of Antony who married his daughter, Juliana). It was built in 1570–73 on an E-shaped symmetrical plan (facing SE, abutting a SW range containing phases that originate in the fifteenth century) using local St Columb elvan with granite for dressings and mullion windows; the gables are thought to be seventeenth-century alterations. The entrance court, now a lawn with clipped yews, was originally cobbled; the garden walls adjoining the house wings are late-Victorian. Seen from the long, narrow Bowling Green.

Trerice's once 'fruitful gardens' are long forgotten. NT additions include an apple and plum orchard with old Cornish varieties arranged in quincunx *fashion – the standard for planting an orchard.*

Explorer 106: SW840584

Trerice, owned by the NT since 1953, is just 2½ miles SE of Newquay. Tucked away in the countryside, it is approached via a winding lane ⅔ mile uphill (SW) from the A3058 at Kestle Mill. Though one of the Trust's smaller concerns, it is a must to visit. Try a fine summer's day when the garden borders are at their best and most visitors are on the beach.

The Cornish Arundell family are of Norman origin (1131) and French extraction.

Ralph Arundell (died 1369) married heiress Jane Trerise, thus acquiring the Trerice estate. Sir John Arundell IV (1494–1560) spent his career in service of the crown, being knighted after the Battle of the Spurs (Guinegate, France, 1513); known as 'Jack of Tilbury', he became Esquire to the Body of King Henry VIII. Sir John was High Sheriff of Cornwall in 1532 and 1541, Vice-Admiral of the West under Edward VI, and also served under 'Bloody' Queen Mary. The Arundells were staunch Royalists in the Civil War, and recovered their former position after the Restoration: Richard Arundell (1616–87, 1st Baron Arundell of Trerice) had fought for the King at the battles of Edgehill (Warwickshire, 1642) and Lansdown (Bath, 1643). His son, John (1649–98, 2nd Baron), married Margaret Acland (in 1675), daughter of Sir John Acland (1636–55, 3rd Baronet) of the ancient manor of Columb John, Devon (the Aclands moved to Killerton, 1 mile E, in 1672). The last Baron John (1701–68) of Trerice married a sister of the Earl of Stafford. On his death the title became extinct, and in 1802 Trerice passed to the Acland family of Killerton.

The 600-ha estate was sold by the Aclands to Cornwall County Council in 1915 and passed through several owners before being secured by the NT in 1953.

Chyverton

View SW over the rolling Georgian ornamental landscape of Chyverton House; in stark contrast to the rust-coloured sandy tailings 'burrows' of West Chiverton Mine (higher left: Cornwall's largest silver producer – nearly 30 tons – operational during the second half of the nineteenth century and ranking first in terms of Cornish zinc output and second in lead). John Thomas, lawyer and mines 'adventurer', created the structure of the garden and parkland between 1770 and 1820. The house is surrounded by a fine collection of conifers, exotic trees and shrubs, and enjoys a sweeping prospect – in classic Brownian style – from the main lawn that begins at the house and undulates down to the small valley and serpentine lake. The courses of minor roads, which form the boundaries of the estate to the W, N and E, were altered in 1770 to enable enclosure of the parkland.

Explorer 106: SW797511

Chyverton is about 5 miles NNW of Truro, 1 mile SW of Zelah and 730 m N of the A30 at Marazanvose. The main wooded estate

(Bracken Woods) is clearly seen when driving along the A30 Zelah bypass at Zelah Hill. Chyverton's East Lodge (Merton Lodge) marks the entrance to the original carriage drive and fronts the old A30 that was the trunk road until 1992. Chyverton House is private but group tours of its classic Georgian 'Brownian-style' landscape garden are available, strictly by appointment. The arrival of rhododendron and camellias began in the early nineteenth century and, in unbroken planting since 1945, over 20 species of magnolia have been introduced by the Holman family in their 8-ha woodland garden. Spring is a spectacle.

In medieval times, Chyverton was the property of the Arundell family. John Andrew of Trevallance (Perranzabuloe)

Chyverton House in plan view showing its pair of Regency wing pavilions; compare the size of the adjacent 'mushroom' of arboreal 'Cornish Red', the first hybrid rhododendrons planted at Chyverton in the 1880s (there is another one along the lakeside). The N (garden) front of the Palladian villa overlooks a vast expanse of grass that falls to the serpentine lake with its c. 1780 carriageway bridge (SE end, higher left) that acts as the principal architectural garden feature. The humped-back bridge is single span with a brick arch carrying the drive that leads through plantations to East Lodge. The variety of trees and shrubs here is staggering.

bought the estate in 1724 and built the core of the house in 1730. John Thomas (1740–1825), his great-grandson, inherited and lived at Chyverton 1770–1825. He was a wealthy attorney and mines 'adventurer' from Truro who served for 34 years as Vice-Warden of the Stannaries. He added two wings to the house, built a walled garden and, beginning in the 1780s, carried out landscaping following the fashionable park style of Lancelot 'Capability' Brown (1716–83). This involved 'invisibly' damming a small stream to form a lake and building a bridge over it as a garden feature that carried a sweeping carriage drive. His first wife was Frances, widow of John Beauchamp (1737–79) of Pengreep and Trevince. In 1800 he called a meeting of 'The Men of the Trees' – great landowners and mineral lords such as Sir William Lemon (Carclew), Lord de Dunstanville (Tehidy), Sir Vyell Vyvyan (Trelowarren) and Lord Grenville (Boconnoc) – who all agreed to reforest their estates, long-denuded of timber for mining and smelting purposes. John Thomas led by example, and with little more than a small copse at Chyverton in the 1770s, he planted no less than 38 ha by 1820 – a legacy much visible today.

Chyverton passed to the Peter family of Harlyn (Padstow), William Peter (1788–1853) having married Frances, only daughter and heiress of John Thomas. After unsuccessfully trying to sell Chyverton, they opted to live there in the late-1830s. Their son, John Thomas Henry Peter (1810–83), who married the daughter of John Magor (1796–1862) of Penventon (Redruth), succeeded and it was he who planted the first of Chyverton's rhododendrons.

In 1924, the Peter family sold Chyverton to the Holman family, of the renowned Holman Brothers – world-famous engineers and rock-drill manufacturers of Camborne. It became the home of company director (Arthur) Treve Holman and his wife, Muriel, who, encouraged by JC Williams of Caerhays and George Johnstone of Trewithen, planted magnolias, rhododendrons and rare trees in the woodland with advice from Sir Harold Hillier (1905–85), who visited in 1929.

Chyverton remains in the Holman family today, their son, Nigel (who succeeded to the property on his father's death in 1959), continuing to plant magnolias, rhododendrons and other exotic species, many of which he collected from seed in 1996 in George Forrest's old hunting ground – Yunnan province, China.

Prideaux Place

The main lawn and (S) garden front of Prideaux Place, largely the result of the Revd Charles Prideaux-Brune's remodelling in 1810. He added the square library tower with finials (left) and the round tower (bowed drawing room with principal bedroom above, centre right; reduced in height late twentieth century), both with Gothic windows.

Explorer 106: SW914756

The imposing Elizabethan gentry house of Prideaux Place stands on high ground 550 m W of Padstow harbour. Its fortified entrance gate, flanked with crenellated walls, is 275 m N of the A389; a brown sign directs you on to a short piece of the B3276 just NW of the fire station and Link Road car-park above Padstow. Fourteen generations of the family have lived here since the house was completed in 1592, and it is still owned by the Prideaux-Brune family. The house and grounds are increasingly open to the public (the formal Italian garden was restored in 1992 with the help of the Cornwall Gardens Trust). The restoration continues. The tearoom doesn't disappoint, and there are commanding views from the E Terrace (once lined with cannon) over the Deer Park and Padstow to the Camel Estuary, Rock, St Minver and Bodmin Moor. The deer park is among the oldest in the country, and still supports a herd of fallow deer.

Prideaux Place was built on monastic land; the name Place is said by some to mean 'palace', reserved for such houses built on religious ground. What is certain is that at the time of Henry VIII's Dissolution of the Monasteries (1536–41), Nicholas Prideaux (1491–1560) bought considerable property that formerly belonged to Bodmin Priory, including the manor of Padstow. The building site of Prideaux Place was a former manor farmhouse and barton belonging to Bodmin Priory (until 1538 the Prior of Bodmin was Lord of Padstow). Before that, it was associated with St Petroc's Monastery, destroyed by Vikings in AD 981 (Pedrog c. 468–564 was the Abbot of Llanwethinoc [= Pedrogstowe, or 'Petroc's-Place', now Padstow]). Before the Normans invaded, the monastic establishment was transferred to Bodmin, St Petroc's Church being built as a shrine to St Pedrog. Nicholas Prideaux assigned Padstow manor to his nephew Roger Prideaux (1523–81) whose son, Sir Nicholas Prideaux (1550–1628), inherited in 1581.

The E-shaped stately Elizabethan house was built 1585–92 for Nicholas, facing E to enjoy the glorious prospect of town and haven. The Prideaux family backed Cromwell in the Civil War but Elizabeth Prideaux married Sir William Morice (1602–76) of Werrington who assisted in the Restoration, was knighted in 1660 and under King Charles II became a Privy Counsellor, Secretary of State and Lord of the Treasury. Edmund Prideaux (1693–1745), son of Humphrey Prideaux (1648–1724, Dean of Norwich from 1702), who is famous for his sketches of great houses in Cornwall and Devon between 1716 and 1727, inherited from a cousin in 1728. He extensively remodelled the house, and in 1741 landscaped the gardens in formal style, inspired by his Grand Tour to France and Italy in 1739. He erected fashionable garden features in the 'Augustan' garden style of William Kent and Lord Burlington: an obelisk, a classical Ionic temple using Bath Stone (from Ralph Allen) and an 'Exedra of Antiquities' (a classical arbour to house Roman artefacts that he collected in Italy). His son, Humphrey Prideaux (1719–

Woodland spring carpet of Ramsons (wild garlic), bluebells and red campion in the vicinity of Edmund Prideaux's Wilderness of 1734.

93), removed the obelisk, preferring the latest fashion of Lancelot 'Capability' Brown, and added the castellated entrance gateway and battlemented wall that greet visitors today (monastic graves were discovered honed into slate bedrock). Humphrey married twice, his second wife was an heiress of the wealthy Brune family of Dorset, whose male line died out in 1769. Humphrey's son, the Revd Charles Prideaux-Brune (1760–1833), inherited in 1793, adding Brune in response to the will of his maternal great-

uncle. Around 1810 he added the square library tower and round tower to the S front, built the Gothic stables and stable yard and turned the dairy into a 'Gothic grotto'. Charles Prideaux-Brune (1798–1875), High Sheriff of Cornwall in 1834, married an heiress of Glynn (Bodmin [pages 144–5]). In the late-1870s his son, Charles Glynn Prideaux-Brune (1821–1902, High Sherriff in 1880), created a Victorian sunken garden, shellhouse and raised Green Walk with crenellated footbridges.

Caerhays Castle

Explorer 105: SW974414

Caerhays is an early-nineteenth-century romantic mock castle with an exceptional woodland garden that is at its best from mid-February to the end of May. It is some 5 miles, as the crow flies, SSE of the A390 at Grampound, mid-way between Truro and St Austell. Park in the beach car-park at Porthluney Cove, ½ mile S of the village of St Michael Caerhays, at the back of Veryan Bay between Dodman Point in the E and Nare Head in the W (these two headlands were presented to the NT by JC Williams, one of the Trust's earliest benefactors of such coastal

A Picturesque view of Caerhays Castle in late winter, looking W across the islanded ornamental lake and parkland, a former deer park. Designed by John Nash for John Trevanion in 1807–10, the castle is cradled in a shallow valley that meets the sea at Porthluney Cove. The shelterbelt woodland around the castle is home to a botanical treasure trove founded by JC Williams in 1903. Look at the scale of JCW's original plantings against the castle's turrets and towers (the slender, impractical turret on the left is a signature of its architect). Caerhays has the greatest number of Champion trees in Cornwall – over 80 at the last count.

SW of the Castle, below the Main Ride, is this magnificent Magnolia x veitchii, *one of several specimens of this species that started to flower at Caerhays in 1930, and is now among fellow Champions. This one lost its top in the ferocious gale of January 1990, when over 900 trees fell on the estate. Caerhays holds the National Magnolia Collection – over 70 species and well over 200 separately named cultivars. Many of its mature trees come directly from China.*

property in Cornwall). The beach is an added bonus and the castellated gatehouse entrance – Bottom Lodge – is a stone's throw away. Less-able visitors may park nearer the castle, still home to the Williams family who bought it unfinished and derelict in 1853. The Castle offers guided tours in season, and the garden – predominantly a twentieth-century creation in a nineteenth-century Picturesque setting – has self-guided routes that follow and cross the contours of this plantsman's paradise. There's a tearoom and a range of tempting accommodation on the estate.

Caerhays came to the ancient Cornish Trevanion family (of Treverbyn, St Austell) in the reign of Edward III, through marriage to the daughter and heir of an Arundell lord. Sir William Trevanion (1470–1512), who married Anne Edgcumbe (born 1473) of Cotehele (pages 152–6), was a master jouster favoured by Henry VIII. Their son, Sir Hugh (born 1500), promoted Henry VIII's Reformation in the west. In the Civil War John Trevanion (1614–43, married Mary, youngest daughter of John Arundell of Trerice [pages 97–8]) supported the King and maintained a Cavalier regiment at his own expense; he died at the Storming of Bristol in 1643. John Trevanion (1667–1740) improved Caerhays and his daughter, Sophia, married John

Caerhays is home to the renowned x. williamsii camellia hybrids, originated by JCW in 1923 when he crossed Forrest's pink C. saluenensis (discovered in 1918) with the small red-flowered C. japonica, planted at Caerhays in 1902. The firsts of the new strain flowered in 1926 and were named after JCW, and another after his wife, Mary Christian. Caerhays is the provenance of these wideranging vigorous hybrids that today number in the thousands of named varieties across the world.

Byron (1723–86, later Vice Admiral) in 1748. She was to be the grandmother of one of the greatest British poets, Lord Byron. The male line became extinct when William Trevan-ion (1728–67) died childless and Caerhays passed to his sisters, Sophia Byron and Frances Bettesworth (who had married a lawyer, John Bettesworth, died 1789). The latter's son,

John Trevanion Purnell Bettesworth (1780–1840) – who took the surname Trevanion in 1801 on inheriting Caerhays – engaged John Nash (1752–1835) to design and build the present mock castle as his new home.

Nash was the most celebrated English architect of the period 1800–30 and a pioneer in the use of the Picturesque in building design. He had established his practice in 1775 but became bankrupt in 1783 when his speculative building developments in Bloomsbury failed to let. In 1792, he became an associate of the famous landscape designer Humphry Repton (1752–1818), entering into a partnership that lasted until 1802. The ambitious construction of Caerhays Castle, one of a series of Picturesque Gothic castles that Nash designed, began in 1807. In typical Nash fashion costs escalated, and by the 1820s profligate living, and an unfinished castle, landed JTPB Trevanion and his son JCB Trevanion in an insurmountable financial crisis. They evaded creditors by fleeing to the Continent, and in 1840 bailiffs took possession of the estate. Nash, however, moved on to greater things. He became the favourite architect of the Prince Regent (later King George IV) and was responsible, from 1809, for much of the layout of Regency London. This included Regent Street and Regent's Park, and landmarks such as Marble Arch in 1825 and the modification of Queen's House into Buckingham Palace in 1826. The extravagance of Nash's design at the Palace, as seen earlier at Caerhays, led to the loss of his position by 1829.

The Trevanion estates eventually came to public auction at St Austell, in 1852 and 1854. At the second auction, Michael Williams II (1785–1858) of Scorrier (pages 77–80), one of the wealthiest men in the county, purchased the run-down estate and the then uninhabitable Caerhays Castle. Michael's eldest son, John Michael Williams (1830–80), inherited, to be succeeded in 1880 by his second son, John Charles Williams (1861–1939), who purchased Werrington Park, near Launceston, in 1882 (his mother remained at Caerhays, and died in 1884). JCW came to live at Caerhays c. 1886 and, together with Werrington, his two gardens were to become hugely significant in the development of British horticulture (hardier introductions at Werrington, more tender at Caerhays). JCW retired as an MP in 1895, and in the interest of developing his gardens sponsored some of the greatest plant hunters of the early twentieth century, including Ernest 'Chinese' Wilson (1876–1930) and George Forrest (1873–1932). Wilson, who famously collected seed from the Handker-

Rhododendron 'Crossbill', a long-flowering Caerhays hybrid (R. spinuliferum x R. lutescens, the latter introduced from seed collected by Wilson and sent to Caerhays in 1904), introduced and raised by JCW and named in 1933. He started to hybridize rhododendrons c. 1895, and made at least 268 crosses between 1897 and 1929.

chief tree (*Davidia involucrata*) for Veitch in 1900, went on to discover fine magnolias such as *M. sargentiana*, *M. sargentiana* var. *robusta*, and *M. dawsoniana*, each of which was introduced to Caerhays where they survive today. And, of course, *Rhododendron williamsianum*, named by Wilson for JCW of whom he wrote was 'The first amateur to appreciate the value of the rhododendrons of Western China.' Among the thousands of 'new' plants that Forrest discovered, *Magnolia campbellii* subsp. *mollicomata* and *Camellia saluenensis* are two notables that were introduced at Caerhays. They survive there today.

Heligan

Explorer 105: SW999464

Heligan is some 3½ miles (as the crow flies) SSW of St Austell, and 1½ miles NW of Mevagissey. Brown signs from St Austell first follow the Pentewan Road (B3273) S and then leave it, between Pentewan and Mevagissey, to complete the final mile westwards. Whichever way you arrive, country roads will add to the last bit of your journey, but the recommended route takes you near the coastal villages of Pentewan and Mevagissey, each with their individual appeal and well worth a visit. But do allow the most part of a day for Heligan's 'Lost Gardens', officially opened in April 1992 and one of the largest garden restorations in Europe. There has been huge media coverage, and hundreds of thousands of visitors to the gardens, per year, since. Though the house is strictly private, this is one of Cornwall's great historic estates with 80 ha of grounds (23 ha Listed) now open to the public. There is much to see –

Facing: The whitewashed, three-storeyed (Mevagissey) S front (actually the side) of Heligan House showing the main block with basement that was built for Sir John Tremayne (1647–94) c. 1692 (remodelled 1810). The William & Mary period construction is in brick made on the Heligan estate. The terrace in front of the house was once a complex of formal parterres, removed in Gray's 'Brownian' landscaping scheme of the 1770s. The Revd Henry Hawkins Tremayne built the adjoining domestic wings in 1810 and, immediately after his death (1829), the main house was 'improved' by his successor John Hearle Tremayne, taking on a Georgian appearance.

The central lawn below the terrace (with larger E and W Lawns either side) meets the head of

Heligan's SE-trending valley garden, a spur joining a series of valleys that meet and drain into the sea at Mevagissey. Originally the Japanese Garden of John Tremayne and his son John Claude (Jack), the Jungle is a steep-sided valley with four interconnecting pools; the top lake is probably mid-eighteenth-century; the lower ponds are early-nineteenth-century. Planting of exotics mostly took place 1890–1900. Now the valley is a lush mêlée of giant rhubarb (Gunnera manicata), yellow skunk cabbage (Lysichiton americanus), tree ferns (Dicksonia antarctica), bamboo, arboreal rhododendron and Chusan palms (Trachycarpus fortunei), sheltered by giant conifers from the Americas, Japan, Australia and New Zealand.

the nineteenth-century plantsman's gardens (Northern Gardens and 'Jungle'), and the productive Walled Gardens that give a fascinating insight into the self-sufficiency – and lavish indulgence – of this grand (once 405 ha) estate that was home to the Tremaynes for 400 years. There are all the facilities one would expect and, particularly for children and wildlife fans, do check out Heligan Wild.

From the reign of Queen Elizabeth I to Queen Elizabeth II – some 400 years – this great estate was the property of the Tremayne family. Tenure began under Sampson Tremayne (1527–93) of St Ewe, a son of the Devon branch of the well-known family. Sampson, although for many years imprisoned under Britain's institutional anti-Catholicism, had acquired Heligan by 1570: first the Manor from the Hals family of Plymouth, and then the remainder, including Barton and Mill, from Richard Grenville (Grenfyld,

Spectacular clumps of hybrid Rhododendron arboreum, including 'Cornish Red', on Flora's Green (left, reputedly named after floral dances held here) adjoining the N entrance to the Vegetable Garden (curved wall of Melon Yard, top right). This area, and The Ravine (1890s, lower right), has a collection of Hooker rhododendrons, or their descendants, given to John Tremayne during the 1850s as seedlings raised by Sir Charles Lemon of Carclew.

1524–78) of Penheale. His son, William (1558–1614), who gained additional wealth through marriage in 1579 to heiress Ann Pye of St Stephen-in-Brannel (where, 200 years later, Cornwall's china clay industry began to blossom), built the first house on the present site and was living there by 1604. Their son, John (1590–1665), owned Heligan during the Civil War of 1642–9, their grandson being the Royalist Colonel Lewis Tremayne (1619–85) who was Lieutenant Governor of St Mawes Castle and present at the surrender of Pendennis Castle (Lewis married Mary Carew, co-heiress of Penwarne). In 1766, the Revd Henry Hawkins Tremayne (1741–1829) inherited Heligan, greatly enhancing the family's fortune a year later through marriage to Harriet Hearle (1750–1805), co-heiress to John Hearle of Penryn. In the mid-eighteenth century, Hearle was Vice-

Facing: View S to the sheltered, walled Flower Garden, with its central dipping pool, one of three productive kitchen gardens and the nearest to Heligan House (top left). It was built for Henry Hawkins Tremayne c. 1780 to produce fruit and tender vegetables, and as a flower-cutting garden. Designed by Thomas Gray – not the poet but an associate of landscape designer Lancelot 'Capability' Brown – the obtuse angles created by the two nearest walls (lower left) that enclose the garden are bisected by a 180° compass line with each angled, 3.7 m-high, elevation pointing towards maximum sunshine. Glasshouses for citrus fruit, vines, peaches and bananas were ranged along these sheltered suntraps, the brickwork facing additionally holding the warmth needed to produce early ripe fruit on trained trees of pear, plum, cherry and apple. Today, a rare 1840s Paxtonian fruit house may be seen, together with an 1880s 45° angled Peach House and the reconstructed greenhouse that came from Pencalenick. The Melon Yard (bottom right), with its distinctive S-facing curved wall, contains the restored late-eighteenth-century Pineapple Pits and early-nineteenth-century Melon House (left), with cold frames in front of a tool shed, potting shed and two-storey fruit store with dark forcing house below (right). The profusion of flowering rhododendron (higher centre-right), in a 'wild' area called 'Sikkim', contrasts starkly with the regimented formality of the walled gardens.

*Right: A Giant Californian Redwood (*Sequoiadendron giganteum*) towers above the tall Chusan palms that punctuate the thickets of bamboo and mature tree ferns around the fourth pond in*

the Jungle. Giant sequoias are the world's largest trees by volume, and can grow to over 90 m high and over 15 m in diameter. The record age is 3,500 years! The chronology of planting here puts Heligan's sequoias with the early shelterbelt planting of exotics in the second half of the nineteenth century (Cornish plant hunter William Lobb sent back a large shipment of seed that arrived in England in December 1853). The palms, bamboo and tree ferns likely date from 1890–1900.

Striking form in an almost silhouetted pair of exotic trees that reach for the sky overlooking the Jungle from the W. Each species displays its characteristic form of tall (in this case 12–15 m), straight trunks crowned by a lofty, ball-shaped canopy: the Chilean Pine or Monkey Puzzle (Araucaria araucana, left) known in Chile by its common Spanish name paragua (= umbrella tree), and the Chusan palm (Trachycarpus fortunei, right), also known from this leaf arrangement as the 'Chinese windmill palm'. Veitch Nursery introduced the Monkey Puzzle commercially from seed collected in Chile during the 1840s by Cornish plant hunter William Lobb. The Chusan palm – the best-known true palm to be seen in our country – was named after Scottish plant hunter Robert Fortune (1812–80), who introduced them, from Chusan Island (China) to Britain, in 1846. Both specimens pictured were probably planted c. 1900.

Warden of the Stannaries and held extensive mining interests as joint-lords of the copper-rich Manor of St Daye (St Day) and of mining land as far west as St Just-in-Penwith. Henry was squire for 63 years, inheriting other lands, such as the Croan estate in 1784 and Sydenham (Devon) in 1808. At Heligan he created the Walled Gardens and principal framework for the Pleasure Grounds, and in 1810 greatly expanded the mansion.

Their son, John Hearle Tremayne (1780–1851), who in 1813 married Caroline Matilda Lemon (1785–1864, daughter of Sir William Lemon of Carclew [pages 69–72]), succeeded to the estate in 1829, considerably improving the mansion and creating the outer ornamental pleasure grounds. Royalties from copper mining – now bolstered by new mines E of Truro (for example, the exceedingly rich Fowey Consols) – continued to shower upon the Tremaynes. It was from Caroline's brother, Sir Charles Lemon of Carclew, that the famous 'Hooker rhododendrons' came to Heligan; Sir Joseph Hooker (1817–1911) was plant hunting in the Sikkim Himalayas from 1847 to 1851. John Tremayne (1825–1901) succeeded as squire – for half a century until the year of Queen Victoria's death – marrying Mary Vivian of Glynn (pages 144–5) in 1860. And so the great family alliances continued. During this time, many of the ornamental trees and exotic shrubs – rhododendrons and camellias, tree ferns and Chusan palms – were planted.

The Tremaynes left Heligan when the house was used as a convalescent home for officers during the First World War. So, too, the garden staff left – off to fight and, most, to forever lie in the mud of Flander's fields. After the war, the Tremayne family briefly returned to Heligan before benign neglect set in, the gardens slowly turning uncontrollably wild. In the 1970s, the house was converted into apartments that were sold in 1983. It was not until the 1990s that the gardens and grounds became the subject of a major programme of restoration under the visionary Tim Smit.

Menabilly

Explorer 107: SX100511

Jonathan Rashleigh (1690–1764) was succeeded by his first son, Philip (1729–1811) – the seventh Rashleigh in two centuries to represent Fowey in the House of Commons. Philip was an expert mineralogist and assembled a pre-eminent Cornish mineral collection. He published *Specimens of British Minerals* (1797 and 1802), featuring many of the finest pieces, a large number of which are displayed in the Royal Cornwall Museum, Truro. Philip built a Grotto (a remnant survives) and planted woodland around the house.

In 1776 his brother, Charles (1747–1823), married Grace Tremayne (1755–1820), sister of Henry Hawkins Tremayne of Heligan, and settled at Duporth. Charles was an active adventurer in mines and built the 'modern' industrial port of Charlestown out of West Polmear. In 1890, Jonathan Rashleigh (1820–1905) and his son planted conifers, cedars, eucalypts and bamboos in the valley, while 2.5-m *Dicksonia* tree ferns – one of several shipments despatched from Australia to Par Station by John Garland Treseder (1841–1923, page 90) – were destined for the quarried Fernery.

The house was mostly rebuilt in 1710–15, its two storeys surrounding a central courtyard. There were once formal gardens around the house but, as at Heligan, these were swept away by Thomas Gray and replaced with a Brownian-style landscape where the lawn was taken up to the house.

Polridmouth Cottage – an estate holiday letting beside the beach – is an idyllic retreat for anyone wanting solitude. The adjoining freshwater lake, now a wildlife haven, was formed when Polridmouth Creek was dammed in 1942, and floating lights were deployed as a decoy to distract enemy bombers from Fowey harbour. Gribben Head, with its red and white 26-m-high daymark built by Trinity House in 1832, is less than a mile away on the SW Coast Path. From there, a two-mile walk N brings you to picturesque Polkerris and the Rashleigh Inn – a 300-year-old former coastguard station on the beach, recommended by the *Guardian*.

Menabilly House lies nestled in woodland 1 1/4 miles W of the narrow coastal entrance to Fowey's estuary and harbour. Its S Front (pictured) is built of Pentewan Stone and overlooks the long, narrow lawn (with great clumps of Cornish Red) that creates a vista of the Gribben peninsula — open farmland dropping to low cliffs and the sea. This ancient seat is still the home of the Rashleigh family who have lived here since John Rashleigh II

(1552–1624), merchant and ship owner of Fowey, built a fine mansion (1596–1600). The house and estate are strictly private, but are of interest as, apart from the historic importance of this notable family, the house was tenanted (1943–69) by writer Dame Daphne du Maurier (1907–89). Menabilly features in the Civil War in The King's General *(1946), and as one of two houses that inspired Manderley in* Rebecca *(1938).*

Tregrehan

View ESE over ordered geometry of the built heritage at Tregrehan. Thomas Carlyon completed the house in 1689 – one of the first double-pile (rectangular block, two rooms deep) houses in Cornwall. In 1770, architect William Wood (1745–1818) added the two brick pavilion wings projecting to the rear of the original house, incorporating it into a larger, S-facing, building for Thomas Carlyon. Col. Edward Carlyon inherited in 1841, and William Nesfield (1793–1881) designed a Gardenesque scheme for the grounds, including steps down to a ballustraded terrace with a French parterre de broderie (dismantled in the 1970s), statues and urns, a circular pond and central fountain that relates to the S wall, and an Italianate entrance court with carriage ring for the (W) Entrance Front. In 1846, the house was refronted as a Classical Ionic villa by architect George Wightwick (1802–72).

The Walled Garden (left, 0.5 ha) was built in 1845 with four quadrants for fruit, vegetables and flowers. Away from the restored, 39-m-long greenhouse range, built in 1846 and once housing the vinery and orchid house, an avenue of Cordyline australis leads past some deep red Acer palmatum to Nesfield's pool – a central focal point of the Walled Garden. The (roughly) N-S axis continues along an avenue of Cornus capitata (planted in 1993). The range of buildings N of the house comprises an 1836 stable block (centre right) and an 1851 coach house at right

angles (behind which is a courtyard enclosed by roofless livestock shelter and larger grain mill). The 1850s pinetum (higher left) contains a range of rare, outsized specimens. Across the Park (where oaks and sweet chestnut survive from the 1680s), an avenue of limes (1880s, top right) marks the entrance drive and lodge (1852). In 1845 Edward

created a formal drive to Crinnis Beach, through an ornamental bridge (now part of Cypress Avenue) beneath the Cornwall Railway. The beaches at Carlyon Bay developed from 1835 when an adit was driven from Shorthorn Bay to take the Sandy river (with tin and china clay waste) away from Par where Treffry's new harbour was silting up.

Explorer 107: SX052537

Tregrehan is off St Austell Road, 2 miles ENE of St Austell, 1 mile N of Carlyon Bay. The house (private) and walled gardens stand on a plateau with a fine prospect of open landscape falling principally S to St Austell

Bay. Its drive begins at Tregrehan Lodge, on the A390 between St Austell and St Blazey, strikes through an avenue of limes, and curves through the Park before lining up with the entrance front of the house. The car-park is to the left before the house; the garden entrance is through an old grain mill and apple store into the walled gardens. The principal plantsman's paradise lies NE of the house – an 8-ha woodland garden occupying the sides and floor of a shallow, sheltered N-S valley. Veteran Champion trees (the garden ranks number two in Cornwall) are complemented by copious newer plantings, many collected in the wild as seed by the present owner. Opening is mid-March–end-May plus one day a week in summer.

The Britannia Inn (where tenants were treated to a pheasant dinner when annual rents were paid) is 137 m from the Lodge and is great for lunch. Or bring a picnic; Tregrehan's facilities are managed by the (very) small team headed by the Hudson family, New Zealand descendants of the Carlyons. They have lived here since 1987, establishing a Green Gene Bank in collaboration with the Royal Botanic Gardens, Kew. Outside the hype of Cornwall gardens' advertising, Tregrehan is a horticultural gem in a fine historic country-house estate, promoted mainly by word of mouth. There is a range of on-site accommodation, and it's within walking distance – less than a mile – of the Eden Project (in the former Bodelva china clay pit on land once owned by the Carlyons).

Tregrehan was part of the Bodrugan estate for much of the fifteenth century. Following the battle of Bosworth Field in 1485, most of Sir Henry Trenowth's Bodrugan estates were granted to Sir Richard Edgcumbe (1443–89) of Cotehele (pages 152–6), and the Edgcumbes remained lords until 1787.

The Carlyons first appear when Walter Carlyon (died 1616) of St Blazey bought land at Tregrehan in 1565; it has remained their property ever since. In 1652 William Carlyon (died 1702) married Mary Rowe (1632–97) of Endellion, gaining extensive property around Port Isaac (mined for antimony from 1723). Their son, Thomas (1658–1724), began building Tregrehan House in 1680. In the 1690s he was purser in the Cornish Copper Company at Polrudden (Poulerudan), near Pentewan, and was searching for copper ore in west Cornwall and in tin setts on his own estate – an activity that proved providential to the family over a century later. A successful lawyer, he acquired mineral-rich property in nearby Biscovey, Carveor and Vounder (tin and, later, china clay) in the early 1700s. The

Camellia Walk, where some of Tregrehan's earliest camellias planted outside used the protection of the outer wall of the Walled Garden. Species include Camellia saluenensis, C. sinensis *and* C. cuspidate, *from which hybrids were developed by Gillian Carlyon: beautiful whites as 'China clay' and 'ETR Carlyon' and the pinks 'Tristrem Carlyon', 'Edward Carlyon', 'William Carlyon', 'The Duchess of Cornwall' and 'Cornish Spring'. The Camellia Plantation was created for many of these, but don't miss the Champion oaks behind the greenhouse – Kharsu oak (*Quercus semecarpifolia, *an original introduction from the W Himalaya) and Algerian oak (*Quercus canariensis*).*

Tregrehan is also noted for rhododendrons, Edward purchasing Hooker introductions from Veitch (including R. arboreum, R. falconeri, R. griffithianum, R. hookeri *and* R. grande*) and planting many of them below the sunken garden. In 1935, Rupert Carlyon (Jovey's nephew and Gillian's father) returned from New Zealand and planted many rhododendron hybrids.*

estate was further enhanced through judicious marriages: in 1715 by his son, another Thomas (1686–1732), to Elizabeth Hawkins (1690–1739, sister and co-heiress of Philip Hawkins of Trewithen [pages 91–6]), and in 1742 by Thomas and Elizabeth's eldest son, Philip Carlyon (1716–68), to heiress Catherine Trewbody (1721–46), niece of Edward Craggs-Eliot (1727–1804, 1st Baron Eliot, of Port Eliot, St Germans [pages 161–3]) acquiring, among other property, Boscundle – rich in tin and copper – adjoining the W boundary of Tregrehan. Philip was a successful mineral lord and owned numerous tin bounds and St Blazey 'blowing-house'. He also developed his keen horticultural interest at Tregrehan. His son succeeded but died childless, and

Tregrehan passed to a nephew – yet another Thomas (1748–1830) – who enlarged the house and adopted Repton's Picturesque approach to its grounds. In 1792 he purchased Crinnis, leasing it for mining in 1794 to the Vivians of Camborne, and again in 1811 to Joshua Rowe, merchant of Torpoint, who struck unimaginable copper wealth at a shallow depth. The mine earned a profit within the next three years of £239,249 (and nearly the same again 1814–33). Copper had risen from £100/ton in the mid-1790s to £190/ton in 1805, and Carlyon copper-mine royalties 1811–41 equated to massive surges of incoming cash. To Crinnis was added those (at least greater portions of) other rich copper mines on the estate: East Crinnis (1820–41 profit = £525,735), Pembroke (1815–39, worked by John Taylor and at one time the second richest copper mine in Cornwall), Cuddra and Charlestown United Mines – the latter exceedingly rich in tin in the 1830s.

Thomas's son, William (1781–1841), inherited in 1830, planting exotic trees brought to Britain by plant hunters David Douglas (1799–1834) and William Lobb (1809–64), much of the material sourced from Veitch Nursery. But by the mid-1830s, William was termed a lunatic – in reality simply a sufferer of early dementia. His brother, Col. Edward Carlyon (1784–1854, who bought Greenway on the River Dart in the 1830s), inherited in 1841. Before he moved to Tregrehan, with his wife, Anna Maria (elder daughter of Admiral Spry of Place and Tregolls), and son, Thomas, he set about remodelling the house and grounds, selling Greenway in 1851. Edward was particularly interested in conifers, planting a great number of species from the W coast of America, South America and Japan. His 1850s 'pinetum' (the name was created in 1842 to denote a collection of pine-tree species) was continued by his grandson George 'Jovey' Carlyon (1855–97), who came over from New Zealand, and from the 1880s formed the nucleus of what became a nationally, and internationally, renowned collection.

From 1898 to 1934 the Carlyons did not live at Tregrehan, but in 1935 Ernest Rupert Carlyon (1892–1941) returned with his family from New Zealand. He was a keen plantsman but died young, Tregrehan passing to daughter Gillian Carlyon (1924–87). After the war, inspired by the old camellia collection, Gillian began a hybridization programme that produced new varieties through to the 1970s and 1980s. Tom Hudson, Gillian's cousin, arrived from New Zealand in 1987 and continues the horticultural tradition.

Place

Place, the manor of Fowey and home to the Treffrys, overlooks the harbour. Clearly visible from the air is the Tudor courtyard at its heart. Grounds, possibly redesigned by the landscape architect TH Mawson (1861–1933) c. 1900, include terraced walks parallel to the river and the curving scenic carriageway that passes the walled kitchen garden with its wavy walls.

Explorer 107: SX126517

Place, the (strictly private) historic seat of the Treffry family for over 700 years, enjoys its spacious setting overlooking the crowded heart of old Fowey. In the fourteenth century, Thomas Treffry (born 1356) of Treffry

Fowey landmarks: view to the S front of battle-mented Place, best seen from the river as it is surprisingly secluded and seldom glimpsed when walking the narrow streets of Fowey. Joseph Thomas (Austen) Treffry (1782–1850) was an industrial entrepreneur who successfully revived the family's fortunes. He began to introduce Regency Gothic to a dilapidated Place from 1813, adding the dominant 'fortified' granite tower in 1841, when two of his copper mines (Fowey Consols and Par Consols) were at their zenith and which, in total, must have earned him dividends approaching £500,000. The entrance hall (Porphyry Hall) was lined with varieties of local igneous rock, cut and polished at the 'Porphyry Works' of his Fowey Consols mine – an architectural attraction admired by Queen Victoria and Prince Albert in 1846 and by the Prince and Princess of Wales (who also visited Fowey Consols) in 1865. Joseph Treffry came to Place in 1786, at four years old, with his widowed mother, Susanna Ann Treffry (1747–1842). She had married Joseph Austen of Plymouth, and in 1779 inherited the Treffry estates including Place; there were never particularly extensive landed estates, and wealth that had accumulated in the Middle Ages through the lucrative merchant trade in tin, fish and wool had long waned. Born Joseph Austen, after his father and grandfather, in 1782, the largely self-made great industrialist and mining magnate changed his name in 1836 by private Act of Parliament, assuming the name and arms of Treffry. His industrial legacy included mines and quarries, a smelter, a railway and fine aqueduct, canal and two ports (Par and Newquay).

(parish of Lanhydrock) married heiress Elizabeth Bonyface (born 1360) who brought the manor of Fowey to the Treffrys. They were Collectors of the Customs in Plymouth and Cornwall, and became successful merchants in Fowey – a fine natural harbour that remained one of the most important ports in the W of England until the mid-sixteenth century. Immediately below is St Fimbarrus church: its tower, the second tallest in Cornwall, was rebuilt in the fifteenth century after being sacked by the French (since remodelled several times). Such attacks, during numerous Anglo-French wars, prompted the strengthening – largely the rebuilding – of a defensive Place in the early sixteenth century.

Boconnoc

Explorer 107: SX146606

Boconnoc, one of Cornwall's most noble properties, and its largest park, is 3 miles E of Lostwithiel, a short, winding drive from the A390: the B3359 from Middle Taphouse is the usual exit for signed events, passing by Braddock and entering via one of the E lodges. Boconnoc house is nicely secluded, protected by its swathes of park and plantation, but its 37-m Obelisk, a landmark in Obelisk Plantation, is visible for miles around. It was erected in 1771 by Thomas Pitt, 1st Lord Camelford, in memory of his wife's uncle and benefactor Sir Richard Lyttelton. The house (empty 1969–2008) has recently seen extensive restoration under owners Anthony and Elizabeth Fortescue, and its grounds will be familiar to those who patronise the annual Cornwall Garden Society's Spring Flower Show, or the Boconnoc Steam Fair. The gardens are open for charity days and on Sundays in May; the property is available for weddings and venue hire, and there is rental accommodation on the Estate.

Boconnoc (Bochenod in the Domesday Book, held by Osferth under the Count of Mortain) was the seat of the ancient Cornish Carminow family through most of the fourteenth century, and passed to the Courtenays c. 1444 when Sir Hugh Courtenay (1421–71, beheaded after the Battle of Tewkesbury) married Margaret Carminow, daughter and co-heiress of Thomas Carminow (1397–1442). Sir Hugh was descended from the Earls of Devon, and unfortunate politics under the Tudors resulted in their estates, including Boconnoc, being forfeited and subsequently granted to John Russell (1485–1555, 1st Earl of Bedford). In 1579, Sir William Mohun (1540–88) of Hall (Bodinnick) bought Boconnoc from Francis Russell (1527–85, 2nd Earl of Bedford) and rebuilt the house. In 1717, the widow of Charles Mohun (1674–1710) sold Boconnoc to Thomas Pitt (1653–1726), late Governor of Madras, who was to be the grandfather and great-grandfather of Prime Ministers William Pitt the Elder (1708–78) and William Pitt the Younger (1759–1806). Thomas financed the purchase through the sale of the 138-carat Pitt Diamond that he bought (uncut at 410 carats) for £20,400 from an Indian merchant

View SW to Pitt's eighteenth-century Picturesque English landscape of individual trees, scattered clumps and the sinuous River Lerryn leading to The Lake (top left) and Deer Park (fifteenth-century, Cornwall's oldest surviving, presently 100 head of deer) beyond. This is Cornwall's largest park with many miles of carriage drives.

(1705–61) and William Pitt (1708–78, 'The Elder'), who became Prime Minister and, later, 1st Earl of Chatham. Thomas Pitt (1737–93, 1st Baron Camelford) inherited in 1761 and made additions in 1771 (including the 20-m-long Gallery by Rawlinson), and engaging architect Sir John Soane (1753–1837) in 1785. Thomas owned much of St Austell's china clay country that was developed from the mid-eighteenth century,

in 1701. He sold it to the French Regent Philippe II, Duke of Orleans, for £135,000, and it was set in the crown worn by Louis XV at his coronation. It eventually found its way into the hilt of Napoleon's sword and is now, since 1887, on display in the Louvre (secondary stones were sold to Peter the Great of Russia).

Pitt extended the E side of the house in 1721. Robert Pitt (1680–1727) succeeded in 1726 and had two sons – Thomas

and was succeeded by his son Thomas Pitt (1775–1804, 2nd Baron Camelford – Tolstoy's *Half Mad Lord*) who was killed in a duel in London.

Boconnoc passed to his elder sister, Anne Pitt (1772–1864, Lady Grenville), who was married to Prime Minister William Wyndham Grenville (1759–1834, 1st Baron Grenville). She did not live at Boconnoc, and in 1833 appointed her husband's nephew, George Matthew Fortescue (1791–1877, son of Lady

View to the E Front of Boconnoc House, its foundation clearly cut as a level terrace into the hillside. Thomas 'Diamond' Pitt added the E wing to the old house in 1721; its extensive lawns had long been a feature. The Parish Church of Boconnoc (on bluff, centre right), in a similar relationship of house and church as at Lanhydrock (photo pages 138–9), has no original tower but GM Fortescue added a bell tower, with octagonal turret, in 1839. The large complex of courtyard estate buildings, stables and carriage house date from the eighteenth to mid-nineteenth century; note the early-eighteenth-century dovecote (top right).

Grenville's sister Hester who married the First Earl Fortescue), as custodian. George married Louisa Elizabeth, daughter of Dudley Ryder Earl of Harrowby, in that year and they came to live in the mansion at Boconnoc. He added many new plantings, particularly rhododendrons, around the house and began a Pinetum in 1853 (today, another restoration project). He also formed the Boconnoc Garden Society. On the (childless) death of Lady Anne Grenville in 1864, the Estate was bequeathed to GM Fortescue. The Fortescues have lived at Boconnoc ever since, Anthony Fortescue taking over the Estate in 1995.

Along The Stewardry Walk (one of the several historic Pitt rides at Boconnoc) there are fine rhododendrons, azaleas and camellias, and a quarry Grotto with tree ferns. The 1st Lord Camelford laid out around 8 ha of woodland gardens.

Twenty-first-century commercial ventures now help to sustain the property, famous as the Civil War headquarters of King Charles I in 1644. Long may its restoration continue.

Pencarrow

Explorer 109: SX0407 11

Pencarrow lies 4 miles NW of Bodmin and about 1 mile from the A389 (Camelford road) at Washaway; brown signs guide you to its nicely secluded location. The magnificent mansion has a unique and truly impressive approach. Old School Lane bypasses the original entrance with its Regency Double Lodges, delivering you into the final stretch of the historic Monkey Puzzle Avenue. The carriage drive continues to strike NNW and kinks through Pencarrow Rounds Iron Age hill fort, now thick with beech, before turning N again into the mile-long Drive. Its linear Plantations contain specimen trees (including many species of cedar, spruce and firs), giant rhododendrons and deep blue hydrangeas. Pencarrow has been home to the same family since Elizabethan times, and both the 50-room mansion – the cherished home of the Molesworth-St Aubyn family – and the extensive (20-ha) formal and informal gardens are open to visitors. Easily accessible, along well-maintained footpaths, there's an interesting Victorian 'Savage Picturesque' rock garden (1831–4, said to be the first in England) with a cave-like crystal grotto (containing quartz and botryoidal iron oxides), a Celtic cross, an icehouse, lake and woodland with many specimen trees and more than 600 varieties of rhododendrons and camellias. The Peacock Café (in one of the seventeenth-century cottages next to the house) serves cream teas, homemade cakes and light lunches, and Iona, Lady Molesworth-St Aubyn, welcomes dogs on the Estate, making it easy to stay for the day in this most charming of properties.

In the Domesday Book, Pencarrow was held by Robert, Count of Moreton (1031–90). It passed to various families, including the Serjeaux and the de Pencarrows; the latter held it until the reign of Henry VII when his unpopular war taxes (particularly the 'unjust' levy on tinners) prompted the Cornish Rebellion of 1497. This unsuccessful protest led to Pencarrow (and other Cornish estates of landed 'rebels') being forfeited. Pencarrow was passed to Sir Henry Marney (1447–1523, 1st Lord Marney) of Colquite (Colquite came to the Marneys from a Serjeaux co-heiress).

View S of Pencarrow's designed landscape: the squarish Pencarrow House and its formal Italian Garden are set in 20 ha of parkland and plantations that contain more than 160 species of conifer and 570 species and hybrids of rhododendron. The Long Drive runs from top to bottom (right), and was planted c. 1842 with Veitch-supplied trees collected as seed from the Americas by David Douglas and William Lobb; Asian species from Nathaniel Wallich (1786–1854, of the East India Co's Calcutta Botanical Garden in India) and, later (c. 1850), from the Himalayas by Sir Joseph Hooker. The picturesque lake, created in the late-1840s by damming the valley, can be seen (top left) with the American Gardens beyond (originally planted with only N American species).

heiress – of wealthy John Hender (1565–1611) of Bottreaux Castle (Boscastle). Their elder son, Hender Molesworth (1597–1647), married Plymouth heiress Mary Sparke and bought the outstanding share of Pencarrow from the Walker family (Lord Marney's heirs). In 1699, Sir John Molesworth (1668–1723, 3rd Baronet) married Jane Arscott of Tetcott (the Arscotts were one of the wealthiest families in Devon under Elizabeth I, the Tetcott Estate eventually passing to the Molesworths in 1783). Sir John Molesworth (1705–66, 4th Baronet) married Barbara Morice

The Molesworths appear in 1603, when lawyer John Molesworth (1556–1634), appointed Auditor of Cornwall by Queen Elizabeth I, took a share in the property. In 1596 John married a daughter – and soon to be co-(1711–35), daughter of Sir Nicholas Morice (1681–1726) of Werrington (and granddaughter of Thomas Herbert, 8th Earl of Pembroke). It was for them that the magnificent Palazzo-style S-facing wing was built, inspired by Italian town *palazzi* (palaces). In 1762, Sir John Molesworth (1729–75, 5th Baronet) married Barbara, daughter of Sir John St Aubyn, 3rd Baronet of Clowance (the Molesworth-St Aubyn family moved from Clowance to Pencarrow in 1918). Sir John had considerable mining interests, and in 1771, together with Sir Francis Basset (1757–1835) of Tehidy, Sir Humphrey Mackworth Praed (1719–1803) of Trevethoe, and his son William Praed, formed Sir

The E (entrance) Front, its pedimented central bay set forward, remodelled in 1844 by architect George Wightwick (1802–72) of Plymouth. Both the E and S fronts were rendered in Palladian style at this time for Sir William Molesworth, who inherited in 1831. Sir William died without an heir.

John Molesworth & Co. Bank. Known (like several later banks) as the Cornish Bank, it financed much of the Cornish copper mining and smelting industry at the time, being incorporated into Praed & Co. of Fleet Street (founded by William Praed and John Eliot of Port Eliot [pages 161–3] in 1802, finally being absorbed by Lloyds Bank in 1891).

Sir William Molesworth (1810–55, 8th Baronet) inherited in 1823 and became MP for East Cornwall in the first Reform Election of 1832 (he was a passionate believer in fundamental reform of the House of Lords, and in 1835 founded the *London Review* for Radicals). In 1834 he served as High Sheriff of Cornwall and, in 1840, as Commissioner for Works he was in charge of the Royal Botanic Gardens where Sir William Hooker (1785–1865) and his son Sir Joseph (1817–1911) were its first two Directors – establishing Kew as the world's leading botanic garden. Sir William Molesworth was

the first to open Kew on Sundays, and by the mid-1840s he championed self-government for the Colonies (he was appointed Colonial Secretary in 1855). He remained a dedicated dendrophile, a passion shared by Sir Arscott Molesworth-St Aubyn (1926–98) who rejuvenated the plant stock at Pencarrow, adding some 200 conifers, 600 rhododendrons and 70 different camellias. He could name them all.

Left: Araucaria araucana, the famous Monkey Puzzle tree, one of the veterans (over 21 m tall) that form an avenue along the 1842 Long Drive. Sir William Molesworth first bought a sapling in 1834 and Pencarrow guest, and wealthy lawyer, Charles Austin (1799–1874) said of its sharp leaves: 'It would puzzle a monkey to climb that', so conferring the common name of Monkey Puzzler (the 'r' was later dropped). Commercial quantities of Monkey Puzzle seed were first despatched from Chile to Britain by Veitch 'traveller' William Lobb (1809–64, page 80). He, like his fellow plant-hunting brother Thomas (1811–94), was born on the Pencarrow Estate where his father John worked as a carpenter.

Bottom left: Emerging from the woods to the rolling, grassy parkland visible in the distance from the long S front of the mansion. Sir William Molesworth was an early Cornish garden-maker who planted his precious rhododendron and azalea seedlings in numerous woodland glades.

Lanhydrock

Formally Victorian, when 'bedding out' bright annuals in perfect clipped box compartments was in fashion. This parterre, on the N side of the house, is part of the Italianate gardens to the N and E of the house. Clipped Irish yews and bronze urns, all bounded by a low castellated perimeter wall, were part of a design by George Truefitt (1824–1902), newly practising in 1854, carried out c. 1857 when fashionable London architect George Gilbert Scott (1811–78) and chief assistant Liskeard-born Richard Coad (1825–1900) were undertaking extensive works, including a new Gothic coach-house. The crenellated wall, with steps up to the church of St Hydroc, was also part of the scheme. Undamaged by the 1881 fire, the N wing of the house (left), with its mullioned and transomed windows, contains the 29-m Long Gallery on the first floor.

Lanhydrock House and its gloriously Victorian Gardenesque layout overlooking the wooded valley of the River Fowey, and backed by a horseshoe of steeply rising ground protected by shelterbelts (view W from above the park and the end of the double avenue of beech that leads up from Respryn Bridge, planted to replace the former single avenue of sycamores. The house – one of the largest in Cornwall – was originally built for Sir Richard Roberts (1580–1634), who changed his name to Robartes. In 1634–44, his son, John Robartes (1606–85), extended the house into a quadrangular mansion enclosing an inner courtyard. The E wing was demolished in the 1780s, and the S (left) and W (top) wings were extensively damaged by fire in 1881. The 1651 Gatehouse (ornamental barbican), with twin octagonal crenellated towers and ball finials, has mid-Victorian walls that form the perimeter to formal gardens with 29 flat-topped conical Irish yews (Taxus baccata 'Fastigiata') that replaced parkland which formerly ran up to the house (parkland replacing earlier formal gardens in the late-eighteenth century). The copper beeches (centre right) were planted by Liberal Parliamentarians: in 1889 by William Gladstone (1809–98, served as Prime Minister four separate times); in 1905 by Earl Rosebery (1847–1929, who also served as Prime Minister). The Higher Gardens behind the house were laid out before the First World War. The S half of the herbaceous circle (top right) was laid out by Lady Clifden in 1914, and the N half by the NT in 1972.

Lanhydrock is one of Cornwall's, and Britain's, great late-Victorian country house treasures – with a situation, garden and park to match. Originally a Jacobean house, rebuilt after a fire in 1881, the property has been owned by the NT since 1953, and is located a little over 2 miles SE of Bodmin. It's only five minutes' drive from the A30–A38 junction at Carminnow Cross – just follow the brown signs – or take the B3268/69 from the A390 at Lostwithiel, via Sweetshouse. A pleasant alternative is to take the train to Bodmin Parkway station, from where it is a 1¾ mile walk/cycle. Allow a full day for the (9 ha) gardens and vast (182 ha) estate with its network of trails through woods, park and riverside, and outstanding 'upstairs-downstairs' experience of the 49-room mansion that exemplifies the Victorian passion for segregation. Expect a high standard of local seasonal food in the restaurant and tearoom, and check out the plant sales in the car-park.

Lanhydrock's history can be traced back to when it was monastic land owned by the Augustinian Priory of St Petroc in Bodmin (there's still a Holy Well in the Higher Garden, once used by Priory monks). At Henry VIII's Dissolution of the Monasteries (1536–41), Lanhydrock was obtained by the neighbouring Glynn family (of Glynn [pages 144–5]). It passed subsequently to the Lytteltons (and their heirs, as the family became extinct in 1600), until in 1620 Sir Richard Roberts (1580–1634) of Truro purchased the estate from Lyttelton Trenance (1565–1641). Sir Richard (knighted in 1616, created 1st Baron Robartes in 1625, for which he paid £10,000) had accumulated considerable wealth through usury (money-lending at very high interest), in which foreclosure of a loan would further gain him the land held as security. The family thus became great landowners and landlords. From their wooded estates, too, they sold charcoal and timber that was in great demand by the local tin mining and smelting industry.

After Richard's death, a great house was begun at Lanhydrock in the 1630s, completed by his son John Robartes (1604–85) in 1634 and completed by 1651. John was the leading Cornish Parliamentary peer in the House of Lords leading up to the Civil War, when he became a Colonel of Foot in the army of the Earl of Essex. In the late summer of 1644 he proceeded to join the defence of Plymouth at the great siege that finally ended on Christmas Day 1644. John became Governor of Plymouth. In 1648, with the Long Parliament in control of the country, John finished the Gatehouse and planted the sycamore avenue in commemoration of victory. In 1660, Lord Robartes supported the Restoration of King Charles II and was later appointed Lord Keeper of the Privy Seal. The male line of the Robartes family died out in 1758 (the Radnor earldom thus became extinct), the estate being inherited by George Hunt (1720–98), six times MP for Bodmin.

George made Lanhydrock his home (ending 75 years of absentee owners), and in the early 1780s pulled down the dilapidated E wing and walls linking it to the Gatehouse, thus, in 'Brownian' style, enabling the park to sweep up to the house. His wealth was substantially sustained through large mineral royalties, particularly from copper mining – principally the exceptional Tincroft Mine where a rich ore body, struck in 1792, had paid him almost £20,000 in dues before he died – some 40 per cent of his entire estate income.

On his death, the estate passed to a niece, Anna Maria Hunt (1771–1861), who was married to successful London barrister Charles Agar (1769–1811, youngest son of James Agar 1st Viscount Clifden – hence the title appearing later in Lanhydrock's history). She did not live in Cornwall but their son, Thomas James Agar (1808–82), who added the Robartes name and arms in 1822, began to take on Estate affairs in 1829. In 1839 he married Juliana Pole-Carew (1812–81), daughter of the Rt. Hon. Reginald Pole-Carew (1753–1835) of Antony (uniting these two great Cornish families) and they lived at Lanhydrock. Royalties from copper mining began to be displaced by those from tin (and china clay), thus continuing to reap a healthy income from the Estate that was nigh impossible by other means. In 1864 the first Miners' Hospital opened at West End, Redruth, on land donated by Thomas Agar-Robartes, who also contributed to the building and was its principal supporter thereafter. The 1870s/80s were peak years for Cornish tin, with high prices and high production, the effect being seen in estate income for the Agar-Robartes family which rose from around £30,000 p.a. to over £70,000 p.a. In 1880, Thomas was a principal contributor to the construction of Truro Cathedral, but in 1881 disaster struck when a fire at Lanhydrock caused considerable damage to the S and W ranges. Lady Robartes was rescued but died a few days later, and her husband the year after. Their son, Thomas Charles Agar-Robartes (1844–1930), instructed architect Richard Coad (1825–1900, who earlier worked at Lanhydrock with George Gilbert Scott) to refurbish the house in the highest standards of comfort, convenience and fire

safety. Tin royalties continued with, next to Dolcoath (where Basset was lord), the largest tin producers in Cornwall being Carn Brea & Tincroft and East Pool & Agar – both of which counted Agar-Robartes among their principal mineral lords.

In 1899, with the extinction of the male Agar line, the title of 6th Viscount Clifden passed to Thomas Charles Agar-Robartes. His son, Tommy (Thomas Charles Reginald, 1880–1915), was

Magnolia campbellii – from the Himalayas (introduced to Britain in 1849 by Sir Joseph Hooker), the herald of Cornish spring. Lanhydrock is noted for its magnolias, the 7th Viscount (1885–1966), who inherited in 1930, being responsible for the mature specimens in the Higher Garden. There are over 120 magnolia species and hybrids at Lanhydrock.

killed at the Battle of Loos during 'The Big Push' on the Western Front (a Pyrrhic victory with 60,000 British casualties), and there are sombre 'tributes' to Tommy in the house today. In 1920 Tehidy Minerals acquired the mineral rights (tin and china clay) of 10,120 ha of Viscount Clifden's Cornish estates, and Francis Agar-Robartes (1885–1966, 7th Viscount), who inherited in 1930, gave Lanhydrock to the NT in 1953.

The remarkable Pocket Handkerchief Tree (Davidia involucrata, named after French missionary Abbé David, who discovered it in Tibet in 1869) in the Higher Garden, a designed plantation with regular walks. Also known as the Dove Tree, or Ghost Tree, from its large white bracts that proliferate on mature trees in May, it was the famous quest of plant hunter Ernest 'Chinese' Wilson (1876–1930). In 1900 he was sent by Veitch to Hubei province in China to collect its seed. His success enabled Veitch to distribute seedlings (1905) to a number of Cornish gardens.

Glynn House

Explorer 109: SX114650

Shortly after the Conquest, Glynn (= valley) was the name taken by the family who settled on this high ground overlooking the River Fowey. The Classical-style mansion, 3 miles ESE of Bodmin, will be familiar to those who regularly pass through the Glynn Valley – either by road or the main-line railway (the old Cornwall Railway, opened in 1859). Leaving Bodmin Parkway station by road you get a clear view of the house, its S entrance front and W garden front set in gardens and parkland; it's less than ½ mile N, just as you reach the T-junction with the A38. In spring you see the blooms of red arboreal rhododendron and azalea in the American Garden.

There has been a house at Glynn, overlooking the River Fowey, since Domesday; the present house dates from 1805 when it was built for Edmund John Glynn (1764–1840), eldest child of John Glynn, a wealthy lawyer, MP (for Middlesex) and Recorder (judge) at the Old Bailey. Edmund, a Major in The Royal Miners' Regiment, inherited on his father's death in 1779 and became a landowner and Cornish politician; he also co-founded *The West Briton* newspaper in 1810. He became a partner in the North Cornwall Bank, but suffered successive misfortunes that culminated in his downfall, beginning with his uncle who manoeuvred control over the Estate by, remarkably, declaring Edmund a lunatic. A major fire in 1819 destroyed much of the house, and while rebuilding was underway the North Cornwall Bank failed, halting further progress as by 1823 outstanding debts left poor Edmund a bankrupt.

In 1825, General Sir Richard Hussey Vivian (1775–1842) bought the shell of the house and the 1,820-ha Glynn Estate. The Vivians were an old Cornish family, one of whom (Thomas in the seventeenth century) married a Glynn. But it was John Vivian (1750–1826) of Truro, Sir Richard's father, who founded an outstandingly successful career for the family as copper smelters in Swansea, where they gained their lion's share of wealth (they had long been involved in Cornish copper mining). He established Vivian & Sons and the famous Hafod Works; by 1820 the firm was the second largest pro-

View N to Glynn House, Cardinham. Notice the ruined conservatory and temple pavilion (centre left) above a lawn which was once the Italian Garden.

ducer of copper in Britain. Richard's brother and partner, John Henry (1785–1855), became a great Welsh industrialist. Sir Richard, however, was a cavalry general who gained honours in the Peninsular War and at Waterloo. He restored the interior and made Glynn his home. In 1837 he was awarded

The Most Honourable Military Order of the Bath and in 1841, while MP for East Cornwall, he was created 1st Baron Vivian of Glynn. The estate remained in the family until 1947 when it was broken up and the house sold. In 1963 the house was bought by Peter Mitchell FRS (1920–92), who won the Nobel Prize in chemistry in 1978; a major part of the house was adapted as a laboratory for Glynn Research Ltd. It was sold again in 1996 and today is divided into luxury apartments.

Rosecraddoc Manor

Rosecraddoc Manor, with its distinctive central bow on the S (garden) front.

Explorer 107: SX268679

Rosecraddoc Manor is located in the Seaton Valley, 2 miles NNE of Liskeard and 1 mile S of Crow's Nest (with its excellent sixteenth-century inn). It is not a house and garden destination as such, but the manor house offers rental apartments together with holiday lodges in a delightful setting of 15 ha of historic landscaped grounds, with lakes fed by the Seaton river. Access is via a ½-mile carriage drive from a lodge off the B3254 Liskeard-Upton Cross road.

The manor house, with its distinctive central bow on the S (garden) front, was built in 1822 on the site of an ancient manor for the Revd George Poole Norris (1791–1869). Norris was the 'absent rector' of East Anstey in Devon, and mineral lord of the Caradon mines a little over 1 mile N. The fabulously rich South Caradon Mine, discovered on the side of the Seaton Valley by working miners (Clymo brothers), was leased in 1836 – sparking the Caradon Hill copper boom. South Caradon alone showered the Norris family with £100,000 in royalties. Fine trees and mature arboreal rhododendron survive as testimony to the Revd Norris's 'American garden'.

Trebartha

View SSW across parkland to a flash of sunlight on the serpentine Swan Pool of the former Trebartha Hall, 1 mile NW of North Hill. Subtle cascades on the straightened River Lynher can also be seen, before tributaries swell this river as it makes its course SE, eventually to join the Tamar. One of these, the Withey Brook, tumbles off the E edge of Bodmin Moor and rushes noisily over water-falls amid the towering trees of Castick Plantation (higher right). Trebartha is strictly private; its hall was demolished in 1948 (after use as a military hospital in the Second World War), and its seventeenth-century formal gardens are truly 'lost'. Its designed landscape, with woodland garden of fine trees and shrubs, is being restored and is open under the National Gardens Scheme.

From 1300, the Trebartha family lived in this Domesday manor. John (died 1441) was Bailiff of the Stannary of Blackmore (1401–05), Bailiff of the Duchy of Cornwall (1407–41), and MP for Lostwithiel – the administrative centre of the Duchy. The last in the male line, Nicholas, died in the reign of Henry VII, leaving daughter Anna Trebartha (1478–1503) as sole heiress. She married Captain Thomas Spoure from Somerset and lived at Trebartha, purchasing considerable local lands rich in tin, a strategy repeated by their son, another Thomas, and great grandson, Henry.

In 1630, Richard Spoure bought Tolcarne Manor from the Kekewich family of Catchfrench (page 160), and in 1675 Edmund Spoure (1654–98), famous for the Spoure Book of 1694, married Mary Rodd (1654–1724), daughter of James Rodd of Stoke Cannon, Devon. Their daughter, Mary Spoure (1678–1728, for whom the Spoure Book was compiled), married Renatus Bellot of Bochym Manor (page 37) in 1697. Mary inherited the considerable Trebartha Lamarne estates, but lost their son (another Renatus, 1704–12), followed by Renatus senior, who died in 1716. Around 1720, Mary married a second time, to Charles Grylls of Court,

Lanreath, who alienated the residence of Court that had been held for many generations by the distinguished Grylls family.

Charles died in 1727, but before Mary died (of smallpox) she became engaged to her cousin, Francis Rodd (1683–1736), and in 1728 Mary willed all her property to him. Francis inherited, and in 1730 moved to Trebartha having married Alicia Sandford of Exeter in that year. In 1763 their son, another Francis (1732–1812), married Jane Hearle (died 1780) of Penryn, adding valuable property in St Erth, Gwinear, Gwennap, Penryn and other west Cornwall parishes to his own considerable property.

The estates then passed to Francis Hearle Rodd (1766–1836), who married Mary Ann Coryton in 1795. They added property in Northill and Linkinhorne to the Estate, but remained childless. The Revd Edward Rodd, rector of St Just-in-Roseland, became his brother's heir, and married Harriet Rashleigh (daughter of Charles Rashleigh of Duporth) in 1805. The Rodds remained at Trebartha until it was sold to the present Latham family in 1940.

Werrington Park

The private Werrington Park, 1 mile N of Launceston, W of the Tamar, hosts Werrington Park Hillclimb and a biannual Countryman's Fair. View over the N park to the eighteenth-century S front of the house, agricultural land beyond. The 20-mile River Ottery (which joins the Tamar at Nether Bridge to the E, right) follows the valley and takes a wide meander around the meadow and eighteenth-century serpentine lake to where White Bridge carries the Drive from South Lodge to the house. The woodland (bottom left) rises to the Terrace where a 3-ha arboretum contains many mature trees and shrubs collected by plant hunters (such as Forrest and Farrer) sponsored by JC Williams. A triumphal arch once stood on this hill, built for either Sir Nicholas Morice (1681–1726, grandson of Sir William Morice) or his son Sir William Morice (1707–50, 3rd Baronet), to the design, it is supposed, of architect and landscape architect William Kent (1685–1748); the arch was demolished in 1883 by 'JC'; other Palladian features survive.

Explorer 112: SX332871

The early history of Werrington includes interesting changes of ownership: 1539 (at the Dissolution) from the Abbots of Tavistock to John Russell (1485–1555, later 1st Earl of Bedford, a close advisor to Henry VIII); 1619 to Sir Francis Drake (1588–1637, nephew of the great Elizabethan seafarer); 1651 to Sir William Morice (1602–76), Secretary of State to King Charles II and brother-in-law to Edmund Prideaux; 1775 to Hugh Percy (1714–86), 1st Duke of Northumberland, who bought it principally for its 'pocket borough' of Newport (which until 1832 returned two MPs); 1882 to JC Williams (1861–1939) of Caerhays, the property remaining with descendants of that family.

Sandhill

Explorer 108: SX427713

Secluded Sandhill now offers luxury bed and breakfast, its commanding and uninterrupted views of the Tamar Valley perhaps best seen in the early morning when the glacier-like form of river mist miraculously lifts to reveal the towering Chimney Rocks in Hatch Wood. Access to the property is afforded by a 230-m-long, tree-lined carriage drive. This is flanked by granite pillars, and

View S across the linear and strongly geometric 'Spanish Mediterranean' water garden (late-twentieth-century) to the little-known Sandhill House, Gunnislake. The house is basically a composite of narrow, late-sixteenth/early-seventeenth-century farmhouse(s) that form the current W range (right), and a wrap-around of classically Georgian wings that form the S and E (Front) ranges with carriage ring. The cluster of structures (top) includes a Georgian chapel (converted from a coach-house), stable-block and walled garden.

marked by a lodge near the top of Sand Hill on the A390 – just opposite the railway terminus of the scenic Tamar Valley Line.

The current house has origins from the late 1500s, though there was a dwelling recorded here in the Minister's Accounts for 1298, on farmland owned by Edwardus de Sandock. A water supply originated from higher ground to the W, and there are some stock sheds and outbuildings that may well predate the construction of the extant farmhouse. From 1790 until 1809, the Revd John Russell owned what was then known as Sandock. His son, John – 'Parson Jack', 1795–1883 – is celebrated as the founder of the spirited little breed of famous foxhunting Jack Russell Terriers. John Senior enlarged the house, adding the Front Range with its central canted bay hosting a grand staircase adorned with Grecian columns and statuary. He also built the chapel, twin six-stall stables and walled kitchen garden.

In 1809, Thomas Wallis lived at Sandhill, though John Williams (1753–1841) of Scorrier had purchased the estate, establishing a connection that marks the property's greatest significance to Gunnislake. That leading Gwennap mining dynasty had, by then, a long association with the area. Together with the Fox family of Falmouth – friends, business associates and also mines' adventurers on an enormous scale – they had worked the exceptionally rich copper mine of 'Old' Gunnislake since the late-eighteenth century. The Williams' involvement was consolidated in 1806 when John Williams bought the manor of Calstock (of which Gunnislake was a part) from John Pearson Foote (1767–1809) of Harewood House above the Tamar at Calstock.

Calstock was one of many manors given to Richard, Earl of Cornwall, from which time it continued to be vested in the earls and dukes of Cornwall until 1798 when it was sold to Foote by the Duchy, though reserving the increasingly valuable mineral rights. In the early nineteenth century, Gunnislake became locally known as 'Williamstown' – the Williamses not only operated the most profitable mines, quays, wharves and limekilns, but supported the development of the village that sprang up haphazardly in and around a hive of industry. John's first wife, Catherine (née Harvey), died in 1826 but in 1832, in retirement far from his former seat at Scorrier, John was living at Sandhill when he married a Miss Edwards, aged 25. After the death of 'Old John', the estate and Manor passed through family members until eventually it was inherited by JC Williams of Caerhays (pages 106–11). There is a memorial in Calstock church to John, his second wife, Mary, and four-year-old daughter.

Cotehele

View S to Cotehele House, gardens and woods, in a commanding position above the tidal meanders of the River Tamar – Cornwall and Devon's boundary – with the Bere peninsula (left), and Plymouth Sound on the horizon. The S Front of the house and its gate tower, and the extended range of the late-fifteenth-century barn (at a little over right-angles to it), overlooks the bowling green that was, until recently, graced by stately 200-year-old sycamores. The slated dome of the late-sixteenth-century dovecote (centre bottom) is sited above a medieval stew-pond in the densely wooded Valley Garden.

The gate tower (lower centre, left), built by Sir Richard II in granite ashlar with fortified embattled parapet, rises from what was originally a service range. An earlier entrance to the courtyard of the Great Hall (centre right) is probably the W passage entrance (centre left) from Retainers' Court. The chapel with bellcote (higher centre left) was first licensed in 1411. In spring, daffodils carpet the lawn overlooked by the NW Tower (c. 1550–60, top right); in summer the terraces (bottom right) below the E Range (remodelled 1862) are ablaze with colour. The Upper Garden has a square lily pond and central island (top).

Explorer 108: SX422685

Cotehele, that most gorgeous medieval fortified house owned by the NT, is located less than 1 mile W of Calstock on the River Tamar. Two of the best ways to get there are by ferry or by train, from Plymouth to Calstock; both provide a memorable journey. From Calstock it's a delightful 1½-mile walk, following the river W before it turns 90° S. If you are coming by car, there are brown signs S from the A390 Gunnislake to Callington road (St Ann's Chapel), or E from the A388 Callington to Saltash road (via St Dominick); whichever you choose, the lanes are narrow so take care. Expect to spend the day. There's the enchanting house (don't miss its Great Hall with early-sixteenth-century roof and collection of armour) and gardens, together with the Barn Restaurant, and the Quay with the Edgcumbe Arms tearoom, the 1899 Tamar sailing barge *Shamrock* and Discovery Centre – from where it's a short and picturesque walk to Cotehele's Morden Mill (which still grinds, and sells, Cotehele flour).

In 1353 William Edgcumbe (died 1380), second son of Richard Edgcumbe (near Endsleigh, Milton Abbot) married Hilaria de Cote-

Delicate snake's head fritillaries overlook a carpet of celandines near the E Range. One of the earliest flowering, most beautiful and rare meadow flowers, its dusky purple or white chequered bells hang from slender stems.

commissioned to arrest Edgcumbe, on suspicion of treason through being in contact with Henry Tudor, later King Henry VII) and fled to Brittany. Richard was back in 1485, and fought gallantly at the Battle of Bosworth Field where he was one of eleven new knights honoured on the battlefield by the victorious Henry Tudor.

hele (1330–81), bringing Cotehele (= wood on the estuary) into the ownership of the Edgcumbe family for the next six centuries. Hilaria inherited it from her brother Ralph de Cotehele, ward of John Eltham (1313–36), Earl of Cornwall and brother of Edward III (1312–77), who was King from 1327. Their quadrangular house (c. 1300) forms the lowest part of the walls (sandstone contrasting with granite above) that surround the inner courtyard. In 1483, great-grandson Richard Edgcumbe (c. 1443–89), a Lancastrian in the Wars of the Roses, was pardoned (of treason in Buckingham's Rebellion the year before), but some nine months later made a legendary escape from Henry Bodrugan (who was

From 1490 to 1520, Cotehele was re-modelled by Sir Richard's son, Piers (1468–1539), who, in 1493 married Joan Durnford of Stonehouse, bringing the Valletort estates, including West Stonehouse (Cremyll) and Maker to the Edgcumbes (much of it being classed as in Devon at the time, only transferring to Cornwall in 1844). They widened the Hall, remodelled the Chapel and created the Kitchen and Retainers' courtyards. Their son, Sir Richard Edgcumbe (1499–1562), elevated the Hall, and almost certainly added

the gatehouse and NW Tower. In 1547–53 he built Mount Edgcumbe house (pages 171–6), which became the main residence from then on. The E range of Cotehele was re-modelled c. 1862, as accommodation for the widowed Countess of Mount Edgcumbe, and the E terraces formalized from an earlier garden. The Upper Garden with pond, possibly a twentieth-century introduction, was created to the NW of the house. The Treasury gave Cotehele to the NT in 1947, in lieu of death duties from the 6th Earl of Mount Edgcumbe.

Umbrellas of Gunnera manicata, *the moisture-loving Brazilian ornamental in the Valley Garden. 'Giant rhubarb' was introduced to Cornwall in 1867, but much of the planting here – including a number of fine trees – dates from the time of Countess Caroline Augusta Edgcumbe (1808–81) who returned to Cotehele as a widow. Her former husband was Ernest Edgcumbe (1797–1861, 3rd Earl of Mount Edgcumbe). At the bottom of the Valley, turn right on the footpath and seek out Sir Richard Edgcumbe's 'chapel in the woods', built on a high cliff above the Tamar after his return to England in 1485; there's a fascinating tale behind its origins.*

Pentillie

Explorer 108: SX410645

Pentillie, Tamar-side and a little over 1 mile ESE of St Mellion, is a charming estate with regular spring garden openings. It is signed off the A388 Saltash-Callington road, between Hatt and St Mellion. Historic Pentillie Castle, lovingly restored, is a buzzing venue for events and weddings; it features in film and television, and you can indulge in award-winning bed and breakfast. Be sure to check out the restoration of the kitchen garden and greenhouses; they are surrounded by a spectacular show of Tamar Valley daffodils in spring, continuing the market gardening tradition of Narcissus. (From the 1880s, huge quantities were sent to Devonport

Pentillie Castle, built on the E end of a ½-mile-long ridge of high ground overlooking the River Tamar as it loops around the low-lying Hooe peninsula, before widening at Weir Quay on its final course S to the Hamoaze and Plymouth Sound. The 810-ha Estate has almost 2 miles of river frontage. The American Garden is showing spring blooms of arboreal rhododendron (lower left) among old oak, beech and chestnut; Ball Plantation (right) cloaks the S slope of Bittleford Valley.

View to the E Wing (Garden Front) of the main N-S range of Pentillie, completed by James Tillie in 1698. There are vaulted cellars; steps from the house down to steep, walled terraces, and three flights of wide ornamental granite steps (eighteenth-century) to the Quay (centre), its cottage and Victorian 'Bathing Hut' (centre right).

market, and from Calstock and Bere Alston by train to Covent Garden in London.) You can also see the three-storey 'Mausoleum' – Sir James's (c. 1700) Pleasure Pavilion and Tower, on Mount Ararat in Hornifast Wood N of the house, and his bizarre resting place.

Pentillie (Pen = Cornish for headland or hill, Tillie the family name) was named by Sir James Tillie (1645–1713), a dubious character who became a steward for Sir John Coryton (1648–90, 2nd Baronet) who built a fine

late-seventeenth-century mansion at Newton Ferrers, W of St Mellion. The Corytons had owned W Newton (Newton Ferrers Estate that once included Pentillie) since 1314, and Sir John's father, another Sir John (1621–80, 1st Baronet), was a politician and Gentleman of the Privy Chamber. After the 2nd Baronet died (poisoning some said), younger brother Sir William (1650–1711, 3rd Baronet) inherited Newton Ferrers. But James Tillie swiftly married Lady Elizabeth Coryton, his brother's widow, thereby gaining land at Pentillie, and considerable wealth. He falsely represented himself, gained a knighthood and, as Sir James, drafted strange interment arrangements in his will of 1704.

Pentillie passed to a nephew whose daughter married a Coryton – the new heir of Newton Ferrers, thereby re-uniting the two estates. In 1809, James Tillie Coryton (1773–1843) commissioned Humphry Repton (1752–1818) to draw up proposals – in one of his famous Red Books – for remodelling the Castle and landscaping the gardens. In 1810 James engaged William Wilkins (1778–1839), architect to Tregothnan [pages 55–8] and London's National Gallery in 1832–8) to implement Repton's concepts. The Castle was remodelled in Tudor Gothic and, in 1812, three new wings (demolished in 1968) were

*Chusan palms (*Trachycarpus fortunei) *are slow growing, so these giants – backed by yews below the E Terrace – must be over 100 years old.*

Pentillie is home to some great trees. Below Lime Avenue, which marks the old carriage drive, there is a row of towering sequoias.

built to enclose a central courtyard on the W side of the late-seventeenth-century house. Until recently, Pentillie was the intensely private estate of the latterly reclusive Kathleen Wedgwood Kit Coryton (1917–2007, an heiress to Wedgwood) whose husband, Jeffery, died in 1980. On her death the Estate passed to Jeffery's cousin Edward, and his wife, Sarah, who, with their children, began the intensive restoration programme that continues today; thankfully now in the public gaze.

Catchfrench

View S to Catchfrench Manor, over Seaton Valley.

Explorer 108: SX307596

Catchfrench (probably derives from Norman *chasse franche* = unenclosed hunting ground/ free warren, or *Cadge fryns* = chief/prince's house) is 4 miles WNW of St Germans, 2 miles from the A38 Trerulefoot roundabout (W of Tideford). It can be glimpsed E-bound on the A38 when descending Clicker Tor Hill (S of Menheniot). It does not open to the public.

This is a Repton Red Book landscaped property. The 'new' house is not to be confused with the romantic ruin of the old adjacent manor house, remodelled and extended c. 1580 by George Kekewich (1530–82), whose grandfather married Joan Talcarn, heiress of Catchfrench. The last George

Kekewich moved away in 1601, on marrying the widow of George Grenville of Penheale. Around 1646, Dorothy Kekewich (1616–93) married Quaker Francis Fox (1606–70), from whom descended the Foxes of Falmouth and Wadebridge. They lived in the old manor house, then moved to Fowey. Catchfrench was sold in the late-1600s to Hugh Boscawen (Tregothnan), and passed by marriage to the Fortescues (Boconnoc). In 1728, it was bought by John Glanville (1665–1735) who built the new house (pictured, with tiled mansard and dormer windows). Around 1780 it was remodelled under the direction of Charles Rawlinson (1729–86). In 1793 Repton created a sweeping picturesque landscape from its entrance front (right), where a carriage ring once existed at the head of the curved W Drive. This involved cutting and levelling a knoll to the W, and extensive planting. Around 1913, under Truro architect Alfred Cornelius (who had taken over Sylvanus Trevail's practice), the house was reduced, Gothic crenellations removed, and the mansard roof introduced. The estate remained in the Glanville family until 1930.

Port Eliot

View SE across Port Eliot's Great Lawn, over the woodland garden to sunlit arches of the elegant railway viaduct that crosses the Tiddy estuary before joining the Lynher river, ¼ mile E of St Germans. Seat of the Eliot family since 1553, the house (centre right) and the grand parish church of St Germans (right again), once fronted a muddy tidal creek, reclaimed by Edward Eliot (1st Baron Eliot). The new parkland, with curving plantations of shelterbelts on ridges to the N, became part of Repton's Picturesque landscape in his Red Book of proposed improvements. In 1802, Edward commissioned architect John Soane (1753–1837) to add to the house with contemporary classical interiors.

Port Eliot is located on the St Germans peninsula, 8 miles from the nearest towns of Saltash and Liskeard, and 12 miles from Plymouth. It is less than ¼ mile from St Germans railway station, and W-bound rail passengers on the 32-m-high Romanesque viaduct (built in 1908 to replace a wooden structure of 1855 that was designed by Brunel) will be familiar with the riverside view N to the mid-nineteenth-century ornamental cannon battery, part of the 2,400-ha Estate. Incidentally, when Estate land was sold to the railway, one of the conditions imposed was that a station should be built to serve the village of St Germans. The great house and magnificent Norman church (incorporating the finest survival of Norman architecture in Cornwall, the oldest parts dating to the twelfth century) are set in expansive rolling parkland bordered on the E by tidal meanders of the River Tiddy.

The well-known Elephant Fayre was held here 1980–6, and the annual Port Eliot Festival 2003–2012. Since 2008, the house, woodland garden (Pleasure Ground) and parkland has been opened in Spring–early Summer for an annual 100-day opening. Whether it's to see the artistic treasures of the 'lived-in' house (there are 14 Reynolds' paintings alone; the 1st Lord Eliot's father,

like his neighbour Richard Edgcumbe, was one of Sir Joshua's closest friends and principal patrons), or to walk and picnic in the grounds (10 ha are, like the house, Listed Grade I), Port Eliot is one of Cornwall's finest historic parks. One of my favourite spots is the eighteenth-century picturesque Boat House, alongside the dock that served the Estate until the completion of the Cornwall Railway in 1859 (in the Middle Ages, Port Priory, located nearer to the church, was a flourishing monastic port). Seek out, too, the 1840s Orangery, and the new Tea Room.

Origins of the Estate lay in monastic lands. St Germans Priory Church was built 1160–70 and possesses, in its W front, one of the finest Norman doorways in England. This is the third church on this site: the first was a small Celtic church erected by St Germanus in the fifth century; the second a tenth-century church, erected by King Athelstan, which became the Cathedral of the Bishops of Cornwall in 926 when Conan was appointed as the first Roman Catholic bishop of Cornwall (the bishopric was short-lived and transferred to Crediton in 1042). Between 1161 and 1184 the Bishop of Exeter established an Augustinian priory and a new church was built on a grand scale. The priory remained until falling victim, in 1538/9, to Henry VIII's Dissolution of the Monasteries. In 1540 the property, then known as Porth Prior (*Porth* = cove or port), was sold to the Champernowne family of Devon. In 1553, they sold the property to John Eliot, a wealthy Plymouth merchant. Eliot created a house out of the monastic buildings and began the park, the property first referred to as Porte-Ellyot in 1573. A later John Eliot (1592–1632) became MP for St Germans, was knighted in 1618 and made Vice-Admiral of Devon in 1623. He had poor relations with Charles I, however, and died in the Tower of London in 1632.

The Eliot family fortune was enriched through marriages, and enhanced by a constant role in British politics. In the early eighteenth century, Edward (1684–1722) married a Craggs heiress of the South Seas Company; Edward James (1758–97), a banker in patnership with William Praed (of Trevethoe) and Sir John Molesworth (4th Baronet of Pencarrow [pages 133–6]), married Lady Harriet, daughter of William Pitt (the Elder, 1708–78), British Prime Minister (1766–8) and grandson of Thomas 'Diamond' Pitt (1653–1726), Governor of Madras, who had bought Boconnoc (pages 129–32) in 1691. Edward James's younger brother, John (1761–1823), was created 1st Earl of St Germans in 1815 and finished remodelling the house in 1829,

Springtime at Port Eliot brings a fabulous show of daffodils, camellias, crocuses and snowdrops.

employing architect Henry Harrison (1785–1865), who had just completed Bignor Park mansion in West Sussex for John Hawkins of Trewithen (pages 91–6) to complete it. Edward Granville Eliot (1798–1877), as well as holding distinguished political posts, was Lord Steward of the Royal Household (1857–66) and confidential advisor to Queen Victoria. Grandson Montague Charles Eliot (8th Earl, 1870–1960) also served the Royal Household – under Edward VII, George V, Edward VIII, George VI and Elizabeth II. Port Eliot truly has noble connections.

Ince Castle

View S across the tidal mudflats of Wivelscombe Lake to the Ince peninsula (enys = tongue of land) that juts into the Lynher, or St Germans, river opposite Antony. It's around 2 miles from Plymouth's Hamoaze and the Lynher's confluence with the River Tamar. The old woodland, with Ince Castle beyond, now hosts post-1960 plant-ings of magnolias, camellias and rhododendrons. The E lawn, to the left of the Castle, was levelled in 1994 to improve the prospect of the river, with Antony Estate (pages 167–70) beyond.

The Entrance (W) Front of the rectangular, brick-built Ince Castle with its embattled parapet and four square, four-storey towers with slated upper storeys and pyramidal hipped roofs. The entrance door, with cornice and pediment above, is reached by a long flight of steps that enter on the first floor. The tail of winter and start of spring at Ince is a succession and profusion of snowdrops and fritillaries and swathes of daffodils.

Explorer 108: SX401565

The lands of Ince originally formed part of the manor of Trematon, which is mentioned in the Domesday Book. They became part of the Duchy of Cornwall in the Middle Ages, but no house was built there until the seventeenth century. On the eve of the Civil War, the lands were bought by Henry Killigrew (c. 1598–1646), a Royalist gentleman from a prominent Cornish family. Unusually for Cornwall, he used brick to build a square, castellated house with four towers and arrow slits – probably with the idea of contributing to the fortification of Saltash and Cornwall against the Roundheads of nearby Plymouth. In the event, the castle was easily captured

Spring is heralded in the 2 ha of woodland and formal gardens by magnolias, camellias and rhododendrons, all planted since the Boyd family arrived at Ince in 1960. Much of the woodland planting, seen here, is around what is thought to be an old bowling green.

by the governor of Plymouth, Ralph Weldon, and never proved of military significance. Both Killigrew and his son died in the Civil War, and during the Interregnum the estate was confiscated by the committee which dealt with royalist assets. After the Restoration of 1660, it became the subject of a long-drawn-out legal battle between various claimants, which was not settled for many years and whose rights and wrongs are hard to discern. Until the end of the eighteenth century, the towers were square on top with castellations, but about 1800 the owner, Edward Smith, added an extra room on top and the pointed towers which help give the present house its romantic appearance. The slate hanging of this top storey was no doubt to conceal the infilling of the castellations. The house, which became even more remote when the railway was built across the bottom of the peninsula in the mid-Victorian period, dwindled into a tumbledown farmhouse. Just before the First World War, Mr Montague Eliot, who was the heir to the Earl of St Germans, bought the house and restored it extensively. However, he did not live there long because he inherited his brother's nearby estate at Port Eliot (page 161). In 1960, Ince was bought by Viscount and Viscountess Boyd of Merton. Patricia, Lady Boyd (1918–2001), who was a member of the Guinness family, was responsible for designing most of the present garden. Since 1994 it has been lived in by her son, Simon, and his wife, Alice.

Antony

Antony peninsula with Antony House (centre right), looking E to Keyham and Devonport Dockyard. Woodland, park and gardens are part of an immaculately designed historic landscape, a luscious blend of formality and informality. In 1792, Humphry Repton visited Antony and submitted a Red Book. His designs influenced the removal of agricultural fences and hedges, enhanced the radiating pattern of formal rides to the water's edge, and created shelterbelts, and open lawns and parkland to form dramatic vistas. Beyond the point of Westdown Woods (centre far left) is the designed, sixteenth-century enclosed estuarine inlet where Richard Carew constructed his 'Fishful pond' (by 1790 Reginald had adapted it as a salt-water plunge bath with Bath House, that survives). The confluence of the rivers Lynher and Tamar can be clearly seen (higher left), together with the Tamar Bridges (higher far left). There's a great view of the peninsula from the train.

View to the N Front and gravelled N Terraces that command a spectacular vista over the Main Lawn to the Lynher river, some 460 m away (these replaced formal parterres and a walled kitchen garden). Beyond the house are colonnaded low wings of red brick (the E, left, cloisters wall carries a stunning Magnolia grandiflora *'Exmouth'), and delightful end pavilions that mark the corners where the front wall returns to the wrought-iron carriage gate. All enclose the square forecourt with carriage ring. The circular red-brick dovecote (bottom left) dates from the early eighteenth century, and from here a 180-m ride through the Lime Avenue strikes NE (out of shot). Aligned with it are the formal and crenellated Yew Walk (higher right), and its range of French seventeenth-century-style gardens begun by William Henry Pole Carew in the mid-nineteenth century.*

Explorer 108: SX418563

Historic Antony – brought to the world most recently in Tim Burton's 2010 film *Alice in Wonderland* – is situated near the confluence of the Tamar and Lynher rivers, less than 2 miles NW of the Torpoint ferry; there are brown signs on the A374 (Antony road). The Estate is in two parts: the fine early-Georgian house and 10 ha of gardens, given by Sir John Carew Pole (1902–83) to the NT in 1961 (but remaining the home of the Carew Pole family), and the 40-ha woodland garden owned and run by the Carew Pole Garden Trust. Visit both for a complete experience of this peaceful and truly magical estate.

Antony has been home to the Carew family since the early fifteenth century (it came via marriage to the Courtenays of Boconnoc [pages 129–32]). In 1554, Thomas Carew (1526–65) married Elizabeth, daughter of Sir Richard Edgcumbe (1499–1562) of Cotehele (pages 152–6) and Mount Edgcumbe (in 1549 Sir

Richard began building Mount Edgcumbe House [pages 171–6]). Their eldest son, the famous Richard Carew (1555–1620, author of *Survey of Cornwall*, 1602), inherited, and married Juliana, daughter of Sir John Arundell of Trerice (pages 97–8. His brother, George, married a daughter of Sir Francis Godolphin of Godolphin [pages 28–9]).

In 1713, Richard's great-great-grandson,

View SE to the satisfyingly simple entrance front of Antony House, two storeys with central pediment, in silvery-grey Pentewan Stone with a hipped roof and dormer windows. It was built between 1711 and 1721 for Sir William Carew. William Henry added the porte-cochère *after 1838.*

Sir William Carew (1690–1744, 5th Baronet), married wealthy Lady Anne Coventry (1695–1744, only child and heiress of Gilbert, 4th Earl of Coventry), and between 1711 and 1721 built a fashionable Georgian mansion to replace the old house (½ mile to the E) which was demolished.

In 1792, Reginald Pole Carew MP (1753–1835), a Privy Councillor (formerly Reginald Pole – he adopted the name of Pole Carew on inheriting Antony), invited that most influential landscape designer Humphry Rep-

ton (1752–1818) to visit and produce a Red Book for the house and grounds (his designs for embellishing the house were not adopted, but his influence in the grounds is notable). Antony's gardens continued their development under William Henry Pole Carew (1811–88), Sir Reginald Pole Carew (1849–1924) and Sir John Carew Pole (1902–93, who reversed the family names). In the 1930s, Sir John and Lady Carew Pole, assisted by the Edgcumbes, Williamses and Rothschilds (of Exbury), planted a 24-ha

woodland garden – the Wilderness – with rhododendrons, Asiatic magnolias, cammelias and wildflowers. Sir Richard Carew Pole (born 1938, 13th Baronet) succeeded Sir John and, together with the NT and Carew Pole Garden Trust, sustains this most remarkable property, taking it confidently into the twenty-first century.

There are a number of impressive trees at Antony but here, on Cork Oak Lawn adjoining the house and forecourt, is perhaps its grandest – a Cork Oak (Quercus suber) – one of England's finest. Its boughs of deeply fissured bark not only reach skyward but, remarkably, extend laterally some 18 m from the trunk.

Mount Edgcumbe

Explorer 108 : SX453527

Mount Edgcumbe is located on the Rame Peninsula, in far SE Cornwall, a jewel in a spectacular setting of magnificent parkland, bounded by water on three sides – Plymouth Sound, the Hamoaze and Milbrook Lake. The House and Earl's Garden are open

View SE to Mount Edgcumbe House, with Plymouth Sound beyond. On the right is the mid-nineteenth-century complex of stables, dairy, smithy and sawmill; above the house (centre) is the recreated eighteenth-century Earl's Garden. Beyond the sheltered deep-water anchorage of Barn Pool (centre left) is Drake's (or St Nicholas's) Island; towards the horizon (higher right) is the Breakwater, with Mewstone island behind.

(seasonal) to paying visitors, while 350 ha of Country Park can be freely enjoyed all year. My favourite approach is to take the Cremyll ferry from Stonehouse, Plymouth. It's an historic journey; there has been a Cremyll ferry since the Middle Ages. The Stables, up near the House, serve great food including cream teas (there's a 'bat barn' too); or, in the Lower Gardens, don't miss the Orangery restaurant (seasonal). The other advantage of taking the ferry is that the Edgcumbe Arms provides waterside dining, just metres from Ferry Quay. There's a network of estate walks you might like to take first, from which you will be guaranteed spectacular coastal scenery – more than enough to keep you coming back.

Originally a two-storey building with a square plan and round towers to each cor-

View WSW to Mount Edgcumbe, and across Barrow Park to Millbrook. Shelter from south-westerlies is afforded by steeply rising ground, above the Earl's Garden, which meets the hill-top plateau and the Deer Park that was granted by Henry VIII to Piers Edgcumbe in 1515 (the landmark W tower of the fifteenth-century Maker Church is just discernible, top left). The steps from the North Front terrace (right of the house) descend to the grassy Avenue and Sheep Park, which falls in a giant swathe down to the Cremyll Lodge entrance and Lower Gardens.

View W over Mount Edgcumbe's Lower Gardens. These are an early, and relatively unaltered, historically important collection of formal European gardens on Wilderness Point: Lady Emma's flower garden, now the English Garden (centre), the Italian Garden and Orangery (higher right) which closes the N side above Cremyll Beach, *and the hedged square French Garden (lower right) with pavilion, conservatories and parterre. The bold straight line of the Great Ilex Hedge (bottom), bounds these formal gardens from the seventeenth-century bowling green and coastal fortifications.*

ner, Mount Edgcumbe House was built between 1547 and 1553 for the Edgcumbe family of Cotehele (pages 152–6). The house is the first major house in England not to be built as a defensive surround to an inner courtyard. It is outward looking, a fine house enjoying a beautiful prospect. Eighteenth-century alterations included a change to octagonal three-storey towers and a W wing (subsequently demolished), while in the nineteenth century white stucco was removed to reveal the present dominant pinkish hue (due to the principal use of reddish sandstone). In 1941, a German incendiary bomb crashed through the roof of the Central Hall – which rose above the side towers – and fire gutted the house, leaving only the stone walls and towers standing. Between 1958 and 1964, the 6th Earl (Kenelm, 1873–1965) substantially reconstructed the original

The Lower Gardens are notable for their Cork Oaks (Quercus suber), this specimen being remarkably upright compared with others whose low and gnarled, deeply textured branches present an irresistible challenge to little children. I, too, vividly remember them from childhood.

The Grecian Garden House in Lady Emma's English Garden.

by King George III, Baron George was created Viscount Mount Edgcumbe & Valletort in recognition, it is said, for the felling of some hundreds of mature trees for the strengthening of Plymouth's fortifications (George was created 1st Earl of Mount Edgcumbe in 1789, on a second visit by the King). The felling of trees, fortuitously, provided an opportunity for George's wife, Lady Emma, to create a flower garden, now the English Garden, with its Grecian garden house. Around 1785, under Richard (2nd Earl, 1764–1839) and his wife, Sophia, the Italian Garden was laid out, together with its elegant Orangery. The square-hedged French Garden, its pavilion flanked by conservatories and parterre with shell basin, followed around 1805. Although Mount Edgcumbe is a 'Cornish' great house and garden, the property has long been a part of Plymouth culture, too; in fact it was once physically part of Devon, so too Kingsand, until the county boundary change in 1844.

sixteenth-century house. Its interiors are now restored and presented in eighteenth-century style.

The gardens at Mount Edgcumbe are hugely significant, and impressive. The formal Lower Gardens (except the New Zealand and American gardens that were added in 1989) began in a former plantation of trees with sinuous paths, known as the Wilderness. Clearance, in 1779, by Baron George Edgcumbe (1721–95), was to make way for coastal gun emplacements – a Spanish and French combined fleet threatening a landing in Plymouth Sound. In 1781, on a visit